CW01430556

PORTRAIT
OF A
FAMILY

Together with
Advents: 48 douzets

William Wyndham

For Roselyne de Fonscolombe la Môle

Defiance (WW for Picol and RdeF)

Now grown up to her grief I steal
Her hope, faith – love ideas
Of time unborn at ocean's Source,
Where peace Its memories frieze.

Copyright © William Wyndham 2024
No part of this publication may be reproduced without permission

Published by Pomegranate Press,
1 Friars Walk, Lewes, Sussex BN7 2LE
pomegranatepress@aol.com

ISBN: 978-1-907242-77-9

Also by William Wyndham:
1001 Douzets (Pomegranate Press 2023) ISBN 978-1-907242-76-2
Two Plays: Cicero & Muso Dosto (Pomegranate Press 2022) ISBN 978-1-907242-72-4
Marching, from the Millennium an epic farewell (Pomegranate Press 2019)
    ISBN 978-1-907242-71-7
Olivacea, Poems 2011–2016 (Pomegranate Press 2016) ISBN 978-1-907242-57-1
Orchads, Collected Poems (Pomegranate Press 2011) ISBN 978-1-907242-12-0
Peers in Parliament Reformed (Quiller Press 1998) ISBN 1-899163-43-3

British Library Cataloguing-in-Publication Data.
A catalogue record for this book is available from the British Library

Printed and bound by 4Edge, 22 Eldon Way, Hockley, Essex SS5 4AD

Cast

GRANDFATHER, Gervaise St Columba

RORY, his elder son

RICHARD, his younger son

MADGE, his elder daughter

MIRANDA, Richard's wife

JOHN, Richard's eldest son

ROBIN, his second son

JEREMY, his youngest son

SOPHIA, daughter of Alys, second daughter of Grandfather

MOTHER ANN, a mother superior

MAY, daughter of gamekeeper Hicks and Mrs Hicks, the cook

AUTHOR

*The 12 characters require at least seven actors: with
minimal changes Grandfather and Rory; Author, John
and Jeremy; Madge and Mother Ann; Sophia and May
can each be played by one actor, as required*

Orchard Wyndham, Somerset, the author's family home, in a painting by the then 15-year old Cecily Perry Robinson. Eric the peacock claims pride of place on the lawn.

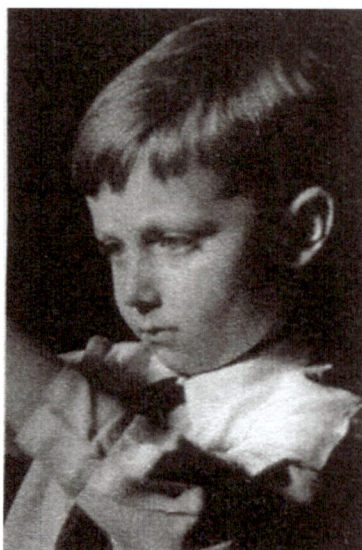

The author young and old.

4

AUTHOR'S INTRODUCTION

*(To be read in front of the curtain by the actor playing John who, for
this introduction only, is dressed in open shirt and jeans and changes
immediately afterwards on stage into John in stage dress)*

I am from an old family in an old house; and an old man: I write
this in my eighth dragon year.

The death wish is the human will to Resurrection.

Humanity is off the straight and narrow. Repentance, I believe,
is impossible in this century, without faith in the Christian
Resurrection to blast off hope. The same belief in their sixteenth
inspired both Luther and the Bard?

The blatant failure of international institutions (throughout the
ages and not just of the Christian and other Churches, the League,
UN etc) illustrates human predilection to leave ownership of our
minds and lives to comfortable corporations rather than to
ourselves.

Neither comedy nor ritual has validity, save out of tragedy and
personal faith. John's miracle herein is his accident.

My state of mind in 1962 terrified my poor parents. I remember
my mother calling down from the top of the staircase to me at the
bottom, that I 'must not storm the gates of heaven'. From that
moment I believe my parents lost faith in me . . .

St Mary's spire that evening pierced the moon next the Sheldonian
in Oxford. So early next morning, I must write to Roselyne and
post . . . What to say, not to sound too frightened? I thought of her
lolling with her sister round their well stonework with high trees
nearby and orioles a-burbling clarinets in the rustling leaves; of the
family chapel where she would lie, down towards the airstrip. But
the organ gurgles in the Chateau's ancient plumbing pipes, she
would know were hers – and needed looking after. That's it, organ
pipes . . . She had already been very ill with appendicitis, when I
met her that Midi July. Beached mermaid forbidden to swim, as
innocent angelic, she had poured cold water down my leg under

the restaurant awning table, laden with a bourride – fish soup with aioli . . .

Good fiction is fact; and good fact may be, sadly – or maybe not sadly – fiction . . .

The Pilgrim Trail
When Cassandra was loved by Apollo,
He her soundings of truth made sound hollow.
    The God by this effected,
    Since they'd both looked rejected,
Blindfold safe alone we'd their trail follow.

But for the overwhelming telepathy at 21 in February 1962 in Radcliffe Square Oxford, after rehearsal of Haydn's Farewell Symphony in St Mary's Upper Room, that Roselyne was after all dying – so that I wrote her a letter in a Paris hospital, that she got to have her laugh the day she died – I reckon I should have gone the same way as John would have gone, but for his accident. As it was, I took my gun over my arm up the Walk into our Blackdown Wood with two plucked hyacinths, pink and blue, to bury near Mother Shipton's Stone – but no cartridges!

(*The actor playing John hereupon throws off his jeans and dons plus-twos and stockings that he wears through to the end of the play*)

PROLOGUE

JOHN *Eclipse at Stonehenge*
For this night, Eurydice, sweat as you sweat at the reaping,
Sweat like the men, my poppy-head,
Who cut and rolled and measured stones to rule our feeble stars,
Stones to encompass your gyre among the dancers,
Till you mirror Selena rising liquid in her arch:
Till you pulse in her to revive her;
Till the wind breathes on the lute-string, but for me only –
That tomorrows I may see patient,
Seeing only your blood on a skeleton of stones. (*exit*)

GRANDFATHER BENDOR – the Library – a wood-fire.
The fire-place (fifteenth century)
Perpendicular is in hamstone carved
As for temple broad-over-arched
To the brain of the household.
And there sputtering gently,
The salamander's tongue,
My equilibrium:
Between the callow leaping yellow
And grey resignation
Lies the full red warmth
Like sap in the roots of the vine,
Stored in the log . . .

GRANDFATHER (*to May*) Ah, come in. I think you like it here.

MAY Of course, sir. I'm born here, aren't I?

GRANDFATHER And here you'll stay. I want you to show our visitors round soon, will you?

MAY If you'll show me how.

GRANDFATHER Somebody must, who loves us – as a guide. For tax, when I am gone, please . . . You'll know about the Watercarrier and the black Peacock butterfly. But the house has a shape to it?

MAY The south courtyard up towards the monks' carp stews and the spring?

GRANDFATHER (*walking May up and down in front of the curtain talking*) They always knew a good place to settle! And when the family came and grew rich on sheep, this second courtyard facing north up to the Channel. You don't need say much: just look! The sea, the sea! But show them the kitchens too and the views on to the gardens. And always ask what things they want to see – furniture or history or pictures or whatever. You'll be quite safe. They always say, everything. Or if they don't, they'll have read us up and will want to tell you! Everyone will own us then. (*exit May*)

Christmas on the Temeraire
Old age: alone on the burning deck of the Temeraire . . .
    I thought, no more to say – how glad I am wrong!
    We lose no Faith but throw It away, my song.
On fire above the land and waters, I breathe fresh air.

    Tugged back to the breaker's yard from facile hope,
My death triumphant but part of me in my elation –
Oh, brightest as sunset I breathe in, lonely in conflagration:
    I am no burnt crisp (lit sister moon, my scope!),

Now first and last I hear the family crackle, their heir
    And cracker: to them I, and they to me, belong.
    With winter solstice in my sails see me elope –
A child with Child and all our loves' new incarnation.

GRANDFATHER Oh, my Helen . . .

We are wanted, My Love – yes, Family wants us! – the lungless
    lame,
  Worn out, outmoded, to man their crumbling fort,
  While they course deserts' cruel desires for sport,
Till finding themselves as tasteless as their lordly game,

  They plunder in dust our archived memory.
Their bones our bones as wisdom's whispering sands recall:
Our anniversary's end's to round their end and all.
  Together piece our shards their history,

They fear them to disinherit, forgetting we are their same,
  Save their course we have completed, as too they ought . . .
  So why begrudge them, as off our parents' we,
Their feeding off our remains, so true to us they fall?

CURTAIN UP

(*A single main set is used throughout the play; but it is almost realistic and requires a largish stage. The large hamstone fireplace in the middle at the back serves as the fireplace both for the Library at the left and the Dining Room on the right with an identical sea view window downstream. There's a grandfather clock in the Library, and both a glasses cupboard and a TV in the Dining Room.*

'The Den' sub-set is revealed by folding back one half of the fireplace showing a bookcase on one side to the left of a miniature of the main hamstone fireplace and folding back the other half to a desk with a bay window view to the sea behind and a glasses cabinet with an old dinner service on the other side. The bottom half of this cabinet has narrow drawers, with two deeper drawers at the very bottom.

Grandfather moves to the Library doorway into the Dining Room, reciting the rest of what turns out to be John's poem. At no time in the play does he leave the Library save a) as above before the Curtain; b) coming to dinner Act 1 Scene 1; c) Act 3 Scene 2 visiting Jeremy in the Den; and d) Act 3 Scene 4 on John's chaise longue in the Den.

GRANDFATHER Nine candles at dinner, but each alone,
Surround by panel oak of a white cloth,
Glasses yet empty-luminous:
Our better angels cast themselves
As shadows among the hammer-beams . . .
A weak sun on wastes of snow –
The power of a candle sinking
The Ark of the Covenant.
Am I past temptation? Bent over
The pinnacle of the Temple
As if downcast, hesitant content
I await the sacrifice:

(Unease for a moment at time past passing . . .)

Jeremy first down to dinner.
So sons make, remake the house;
Suns rise and set; so space between dreams is filled.

   Mother Julian, who lived in a cell,
   Said all manner of things shall be well.
      How on Earth would she know?
      So to heaven she'd go,
   From where we make of heaven our hell.

ACT 1, SCENE 1

(Christmas Eve. John and Sophia are finishing the Christmas tree in the Library. They then hurry into the Dining Room)

JOHN Now the green man for the centre over the table and the glasses for May. Have you seen the cellar? Rows and rows like a regiment on parade. In the Library Grandfather mainly sleeps; but I bet his thoughts are on those bottles and the sunlight stored in them. His Library and his cellar: I sometimes wonder if he cares for anything else.

SOPHIA There's more to Grandfather than that. It takes time to collect wisdom, books and wine. We must get something out of growing old. When you're a very old man, you can tell me all about wine, and whether you've learnt anything. (*John pretends to push her off the steps*) Here, you do it: I can't reach. He should go first and on the tree I think, really. But he is Bendor at Christmas after all. So he can be the final touch. Why do you think I remember only him here from five years ago?

JOHN He is a family tradition you won't see anywhere else. And maybe you connect his evergreen with Grandfather? Think of that Saxon Oak: he has lost all the branches. It's just a huge hollow stump, but the leaves sprout just the same on top. And the tree guards its spirit even at the low point of winter, an ember to light the fire next morning. I gave him my poem.

SOPHIA (*nodding*) I liked the bit about the angels in the beams.

JOHN 'The Cutting of the Cake' – horribly banal title. I shall have to think of something better.

SOPHIA Nice poem, though. You do the glasses? I've a present for him too. Before the others come down.

JOHN (*laughs*) No sense of style or just lazy? All right.

SOPHIA I hate laying tables. Like a chess board – as if every game has to start out the same. (*exit*)

(*John looks at the Green Man over the table and out to sea, walks slowly over to the glass cupboard*)

JOHN Oh, good. Come in, May, and I'll show you which glasses.

(*May is not seen. Sophia joins Grandfather in the Library, while John decants the wine and exits*)

SOPHIA Grandfather, I have something for you.

GRANDFATHER Something for me, wise child?

SOPHIA Not fair to tease. And you are wise.

GRANDFATHER If so, maybe because I have been here a surprisingly long time.

SOPHIA Every wood fire is different.

GRANDFATHER Like sunsets.

(*Grandfather sits Sophia down by a good fire and tries on his present – slippers. Then between puffs at his pipe*)

GRANDFATHER They do fit – this room and all that's left of me. No brogues for me now. But among old books. They are like Papa's old trench coat: not wearing it outside in winter, I felt incomplete. As you might come to like those in your room? They are for you.

SOPHIA No, surely?

(*Grandfather points to two water colours. Sophia puts on a light to look, awkwardly*)

SOPHIA Why me?

GRANDFATHER I caught them just before the Great War in an Oxford antique den. Gave them to brother Raymond going out to fight, for his collection. At the start I wasn't quite old enough. Fine man – and we've a few of his war sketches. He died and I survived. Your painting going all right?

SOPHIA (*curtly, but nervous, not meaning to be rude*) No!

GRANDFATHER You'll find plenty here to look at and cut your teeth on. Living here will suit you, I think. You are not like your Mama, who used to think life would always begin over the next mountain.

SOPHIA (*slowly*) Please don't talk of her like that – so as to analyse her. Whatever even I say about her, nice or nasty, never sounds more than a half-truth. So I never know quite what to think. She did love me, too much I think: she couldn't bear me not to be there. But after Gerald – Father, sorry – or rather to start with, first there was Charles. He was rather nice and was always giving me presents, to make Father and Alys – oh dear, sorry, Mama – simultaneously jealous. He lasted quite a long time. Next came her casuals, she called them. They were all pilots – airline and military – or racing drivers, who could give her travel and/or thrills. I wish I knew where she found them all. Until I was almost glad of her accident. Well, no of course I wasn't, no. But everything for her was an accident, probably including me. That one was just her last . . .. So do you think my life will start here?

GRANDFATHER (*laughing*) Your life is almost a quarter over. If I am not to talk of Alys – which is a bit hard, she was my daughter, you know – you must take care not to be like her. Bendor is not your first mountain, nor even your next mountain, but this mountain from which to survey us and perhaps yourself.

SOPHIA You are sounding like the Tempter showing me the whole world laid out here for me at my feet, like in John's poem. But like my mother I am not past temptation. Perhaps I'd rather stay young and never be wise, after all.

GRANDFATHER (*musing*) Which is precisely the choice Alys made.

(*Enter Robin*)

ROBIN Happy birthday, Grandad. Hello, Sophia. (*He helps himself to Grandfather's whiskey*) Hope you don't mind, since it's yours. Father doesn't have Irish.

GRANDFATHER No, no. Help yourself.

SOPHIA As you always do.

ROBIN Oh, sorry. You're not drinking yet? (*Drinks with satisfaction*) How are we settling in? Liking Bendor more than Alys did?

GRANDFATHER Aunt Alys!

ROBIN Sophia calls her Alys.

SOPHIA (*quickly*) Not with Grandfather.

(*Enter Rory with a tray of drinks via the Dining Room – that's to say, he is seen leaving the Dining Room by edge of stage door, then re-appearing at the Library twin door on the other end of the stage. This throughout is the way from Dining Room to Library and back*)

RORY Here we are – a present from Miranda upstairs. (*sees Robin*) I see you have made yourself at home!

GRANDFATHER I said he could.

(*Robin, without asking, hands Grandfather a glass of Irish and holds the sherry bottle out to Sophia – who nods – pours two glasses and sits down*)

ROBIN (*loudly*) A fine night for pigeon – windy, cold. Had sixteen with twenty-five cartridges.

GRANDFATHER I thought I heard you; but where were you?

ROBIN In Lime Spinney. Yes, I know (*defensively*), it is a bit close to Sampson Wood. But Father said it shouldn't disturb the pheasants too much.

RORY I see. But it is *my* job to run the Estate. That means . . .

(*Enter Richard via the Dining Room with John unnoticed behind him. Robin is at once on his feet, giving his father a Scotch from the tray. Richard sits beaming in the chair that Robin has just vacated for him*)

RICHARD Thanks. You have been to a good school. You know he was captain, Sophia – of damn near everything.

JOHN It was all very splendid.

ROBIN Only luck, I expect.

SOPHIA I expect so.

GRANDFATHER There are diversities of gifts.

(*An awkward pause in the Library: but meanwhile Miranda has entered the Dining Room, fussily checks the table, looks up at the green man and alters a few objects on the tree*)

RICHARD (*bending towards her through an imaginary door and laughing*) You look as though you are arranging your hair.

MIRANDA All ready I think.

RICHARD Hadn't even finished my drink. Any luck, Robin?

ROBIN Three bags full, and a right and left.

JOHN (*to Sophia*) Robin always shoots them flying. Much more difficult.

(*All are moving through to the Dining Room*)

SOPHIA (*with her head in the Dining Room curtains*) Snow – an ocean round and above us. And soon silent footsteps.

JOHN In a new world.

RICHARD (*to Robin*) Lucky you got out this afternoon.

JOHN (*to Sophia*) And you came in time. (*exit*)

RORY Miranda, the table does look nice. Father's birthday, but your Christmas.

MIRANDA My thanks, noble lord.

GRANDFATHER (*seeing Jeremy hovering*) May I have Jeremy on my right?

MIRANDA Whatever has become of Madge?

GRANDFATHER I do hope it's not her neck. It has never been right since Boreas . . .

ROBIN I think she was lucky not to break it. I saw her, going like a Cossack.

SOPHIA It was more Mrs Hicks and the pheasant casserole. Auntie Madge did the plucking. But she assured me she would be down.

JOHN (*hovering in the doorway*) I'll go again and fetch her.

RICHARD Good old Madge. I talk, you talk, she works. Bendor's regular verb!

(*The lights dim to the bare candles as Madge comes in with John and joins the others sitting down. Then as the lights go up again, all are standing. May is seen entering with the coffee tray and clearing plates. Jeremy helps and exits with her*)

GRANDFATHER Now for the tree, I think.

(*The family move quickly into the Library*)

ROBIN Game always tastes best when you shot it yourself.

RICHARD But not when you plucked it, eh, Madge?

JEREMY (*re-entering pompously with Sophia*) Tomorrow, Sophia, you and I shall beat the bounds.

GRANDFATHER (*to Sophia*) We don't hunt now since Aunt Madge's accident. And anyway horses are expensive. So this beating the bounds is Jeremy's version of a Boxing Day meet, I suppose. He means, young lady, you see the family's remaining domain – an honour. (*to Jeremy*) I thought you always go alone.

JEREMY This is chivalry and different; and I don't see why Sophia should wait for my birthday to be shown all roundabout. (*To Sophia*)

You see on my birthday, the first of August, easy to remember –
which is actually the Swiss national day, so when I was young,
you, Grandpa, used to call me William Tell . . .

ROBIN End of fourth bracket . . .

JEREMY On my birthday, Sophe, I am up at dawn and away. I have
a ceremonial route past the old farm buildings and along the river,
north down to the Channel. Then along the shore to the foot of
Puxtor – that's Puck, our friend too, you know. A run up his Tor
steep and over and down the other side. This gets you up river to
Heron Island in the river. So – round the island in Seagull.

ROBIN Father's boat.

JEREMY And so to breakfast.

MADGE (*with a boisterous laugh*) And no one will suggest this time
you swam round.

JEREMY This shall be your Rite of Bendor.

SOPHIA Thanks. Christmas sounds a nice time to do it. But Seagull
looks like a duck breast upturned in a soup plate. Ice in and out,
like a Dutch winter scene.

RORY Even so, no one please is ever to bathe in that stretch of river:
there are rocks and even whirlpools.

RICHARD However it has been credibly suggested (*an approving
glance at Robin*) that our athletic Jeremy could never have taken
three hours for his birthday ritual if he had taken my boat . . . The
estate is not what it used to be – despite what Father has done for
us.

GRANDFATHER One is only 80 once.

(*Exit. The others follow Grandfather out of the Dining Room into the Library, where Grandfather does not at once appear*)

ROBIN (*loudly*) Furthermore Bottom . . .

MADGE Uncle Richard's new spaniel.

SOPHIA I know. I've walked him.

ROBIN . . . was not wet with sea water.

JEREMY Shut up, sneak! (*exit*)

SOPHIA (*to Richard*) It's nice idea of Jeremy's. But the pond is frozen hard. Perhaps we can skate? (*to John, entering*) Remember Oxford - the Cherwell and the Leg of Mutton pond – last winter. Up, around and down . . . And the willows, crouched like witches, watching, watching, the dance?

JOHN Yes – and that was the last time I saw Auntie Alys.

ROBIN It is unlucky to even refer to Macbeth.

RORY Split infinitive!

RICHARD I think Sophia was thinking of Romeo and Juliet.

RORY There are no witches in Romeo and Juliet.

ROBIN (*vaguely*) I thought there was a dance. In the film anyway.

JOHN I cannot make sense of Shakespeare as a whole. There seems no connect between the comedies and the deep tragedies. He seems to kill off his sweetest characters for the hell of it. Neither Cordelia nor Juliet need have died. Ophelia is pretty – and pretty well irrelevant.

RICHARD He called Romeo and Juliet a tragedy; so his audience had to expect a tragedy. But what's in a name?

RORY And Desdemona? Without her death, no Othello.

JOHN OK. I sentence Desdemona to death.

RORY The Bard I think could not reconcile, as he thought his England, his Gloriana – and probably his Comedy – needed, Protestant and Catholic London. In the end, in my favourites, A Winter's Tale and The Tempest, he gives up: God everywhere . . .

> Cordelia's to martyr born, if honest's too true to live.
>> Where's justice not with Paulina's virtue blent?
>> Ophelia's but tool of baseness, since innocent.
> Her love to artless soldier may Desdemona give?

> Paulina but seeded a man his sins to atone
> With good; nor Hamlet his father's killer to eternity
> Must judge: thus Claudius to judge himself left free.
>> However play men or women, their Soul's Its own;

> All history, man's garden his fare to cull and sieve.
>> Who clothes with grace the body mends not the intent.
>> In congregation none lonely; but pilgrim's alone.
> No saint but in Company; no Church may conscience be.

RICHARD A Church for the Bard: my brother's explanation of why he is not a Catholic – nor anything else much!

(*An awkward silence, Rory exit looking angry*)

ROBIN (*to Sophia*) If you like, you can stand with me on Grand Day. We always have the shoot to ourselves then. Grandfather says we had to syndicate the other days; and I end up placing the guns. But unlike me, John always shoots, don't you, John? But on Grand Day we both do.

SOPHIA Perhaps I can take it in turns with you and John?

MADGE (*smiling*) Let the ballet commence!

ROBIN On ice.

(*Re-enter Grandfather, who unwraps a bottle and gives it to John*)

GRANDFATHER Green Chartreuse – apologia for Catholicism, I rather think – and the only possible accompaniment for Madge's plum cake. Thank you, Madge. Please do the honours.

(*Madge cuts the cake and leaves it in portions on Grandfather's desk. John collects glasses from the Dining Room.*)

JOHN Actually Grandfather, my poem, the one I wrote for you: may I read it?

GRANDFATHER I have read it – aloud to myself, as I like. But I'll read it again.

(*He takes a sheet and reads to himself*)

RICHARD Don't be ridiculous – and pretentious – John. Even Rory gave up writing poetry at twenty. His tutor told him, I remember, no one has a new idea after that.

ROBIN Uncle Rory says, writing poetry wasn't encouraged in the Seminary. Vide Hopkins!

GRANDFATHER (*finishing reading and handing round the cake*) Thank you, John, very much.

ROBIN Father, Grandfather, don't you think a toast?

GRANDFATHER Well, now why not? Now Miranda, may I? (*Lifts his glass*)

RICHARD I suppose that is to be celebrated.

GRANDFATHER (*with an eye on Miranda*) To a tenth candle a table.

SOPHIA Auntie Miranda, how lovely. When? (*She jumps up to kiss her*)

MIRANDA Soon after Easter

ALL A tenth candle!

RICHARD (*coldly*) I was meaning The Toast.

GRANDFATHER (*dangerously quietly*) I see. But our second toast may not be quite what you think.

GRANDFATHER (*lifting his glass again*) The Devil take the Exciseman!

ALL The Devil take the Exciseman!

RICHARD A capital toast! (*Then quietly to Grandfather*) It is the seven years and the Devil has got 'im?

GRANDFATHER Yes.

RICHARD So Bendor belongs to Rory, me, Madge and Sophia (as Alys' heir) for our lifetimes and to my children after? And your shares too?

GRANDFATHER The house, yes. But I'm afraid all those years ago I spoke loosely: by Bendor I meant the house. Rory, as my eldest, was still in the Kenya Mission, remember. And I didn't want the rump of our land split up. The shares must support the shrinking estate as a whole.

RICHARD I have been hoping you'd be thinking of that. Father, I congratulate you. So naturally I . . ?

GRANDFATHER (*kindly and quietly*) No! The land is John's. Jeremy must be sure to ask John's permission beating the bounds tomorrow!

SOPHIA Oh, John!

ROBIN And I thought I was going to read agriculture!

RICHARD (*looking Grandfather hard in the eye*) Your set, Father, I think.

GRANDFATHER I never did much like toasts, Miranda, my dear. And I do seem rather to have been the centre of the stage. Will you very kindly for a change do the tree for us?

(*Sophia whispers in Miranda's ear, then runs from the Library gathering to the Dining Room, climbs on the table and with a jerk dislodges the Green Man and runs back into the Library to present him to Grandfather. Miranda meanwhile is rummaging helplessly with the presents under the tree.*)

MIRANDA I do wish people could write more clearly.

MADGE I'll do it.

MIRANDA But your neck, bending?

23

MADGE Hang my neck. (*She is already sorting the parcels in neat piles*) And you're pregnant. (*Getting up with a flourish*) People collect their own. I think they are all labelled who they are from. That's what I like about Christmas: at least there we all know what we are about!

(*During the next sequence presents are opened and thanks given*)

MADGE Something for everyone and generally not what they want. Like any other day of the year.

JOHN (*to Grandfather*) Oh, more Chartreuse? What has Jeremy got?

RICHARD An outboard for Seagull. He will be fiddling with it in the boathouse.

GRANDFATHER (*to Sophia*) Spoil me, my dear. Will you bring me mine? (*Falling back into his armchair, tired*) Thankyou.

SOPHIA (*opening hers from Grandfather*) You're spoiling me. Scent! Mmm . . . (*She offers a sniff to Madge*)

RICHARD (*Grinning at Madge, who obviously never uses scent*) Not for you? Exception for Christmas?

MADGE (*getting cross*) Not even at Christmas. Ah, but this? Thank you, Father! (*holding up a bulky necklace of black and gold chips: attractive and expensive*) It suits me. Why do I like it so especially?

SOPHIA Because Grandpa gave it? The Bendor colours, black and gold.

ROBIN Basalt chips off the future?

MIRANDA Amber from the past.

24

RICHARD So where's the fly in the ointment, Miranda, my love?

MADGE (*with a loud laugh*) Always in your nasty mind, dear brother.

ROBIN Oh, look! John has got two of the same – Oxford Dictionary of Quotes. Can I look up Romeo and Juliet?

RICHARD Who are they from?

JOHN Mother and Uncle Rory.

RICHARD I am surprised they didn't get together. We're used to more effective co-operation. Around Easter, didn't you say, my love?

GRANDFATHER (*suddenly on his feet*) That, Richard, isn't funny.

RICHARD It wasn't intended to be. We're still your schoolboys here, Father. (*Looking at Robin*) Second set to me.

GRANDFATHER Very well. (*He calmly turns off the tree and then, one by one, all the other lights*) Good night everybody. Thank you, Richard, for a happy birthday.

(*Bewildered, all leave the room, one by one, Sophia blowing Grandfather a kiss second last. Last Sophia kisses over her shoulder to Madge*)

MADGE You see, Christmas is a birthday, just like all the other days. And Father's the same.

End Act 1, Scene 1

25

(The Den. A low dingy ground floor room with ugly book cases untidily filled. In one corner a pile of papers and notes. No desk in use but a table covered with fountain pens, ink bottles and pencils, an electric kettle and mugs. Though cluttered, the room looks half-heartedly tidied, but has two redeeming features, a small hamstone fireplace (wood fire dying down) and a bay window, with seats and mistletoe suspended from a disused light socket, that looks downriver to sea. There are sprigs of holly around and a door half hiding rough steps to an attic. However, now not much more than fire and moon-lit bay window are shown clear.)

(A soft knock)

JOHN You're late; and the fire is almost out. (*Sophia enters and pretends to make off*) Here – bless Grandpa: do you want his Chartreuse or a last sniff of my birthday brandy? It's almost up in smoke. Silly me: I thought you'd be on the stroke of Christmas and it's overwarmed.

SOPHIA You do go on. (*takes the brandy and sinks her face into the bowl glass*) The air's heavy with it. Lovely. But isn't 21 a bit early to be a confirmed bachelor?

JOHN Let me reassure you. There are the logs; here's the fire.

SOPHIA (*making up the fire*) Even Sherlock had a housekeeper. And Grandpa has Mrs Hicks. By the way, isn't it odd that Auntie Madge, not Auntie Miranda, runs things here?

JOHN Horses for courses. Mama is decorative. Auntie Madge is horse-faced, and *was* horsey until she fell off.

SOPHIA Cad! Like Uncle Rory runs the estate, though your Papa is not decorative. Though I suppose Rory is the elder brother.

JOHN Papa did it before Uncle Rory left the Mission.

SOPHIA Golly! (*looking through the brandy bowl at the blaze*) I hope the Den doesn't blow up – like a refinery.

JOHN I guess a holocaust is just possible.

SOPHIA (*leaning forward and imitating Richard*) Father, don't you think – a toast? (*They laugh*)

JOHN I didn't mean that. Don't let's be like them. What do *you* think of them?

SOPHIA I like Auntie Madge – Medusa wisps waving in squalls of laughter. And of course Grandpa. But don't let's talk of them. Am I to be shown round or not?

JOHN You should be in bed.

SOPHIA So I was, when Auntie Madge hung up my stocking.

JOHN You wouldn't burn my books?

SOPHIA I'll burn those essays over there, if they're bad.

JOHN How would you know? You have little Latin and less Greek.

SOPHIA I don't hold with the occult sciences.

JOHN Coward! We have to lay Bendor's ghosts.

SOPHIA Then we must start with cupboards and find the skeletons. What's in *there*?

JOHN That's the attic. You go.

(Sophia goes up, chattering and occasionally looking and gesticulating round the door of the stairway. John stays sitting at the fire)

SOPHIA Wrought-iron fenders, saddles and stirrups and this lovely fishing rod. And family photos – they always frighten me – latter-day fossils. And look here. *(waving a little black book)* 'Today in the Kingdom of Heaven'.

JOHN And here we are. Well, it *is* Christmas Day . . . Must be Granny Helen's.

SOPHIA But this is like an archaeological dig, level under level.

JOHN Stratum upon stratum. Do you see here the glass cabinet, the one with shallow drawers? Old porcelain displayed above, lepidoptera below it; and at the bottom two big drawers: Uncle Raymond's worldly goods, and in particular his collection of butterflies. *That* Uncle Raymond was my grandfather's uncle. Those poor pinned beauties were to be for his masterpiece, Butterflies of Somerset. Somersette Ealle. He never even started writing.

SOPHIA They are quite lovely where they are. But like photos, dead.

JOHN 'Gathered flowers are dead, Yasmin.' But here – now see this. *(Sophia comes down the steps as he takes a glass-fronted cigar box out of a drawer)* This is the Black Peacock. Very rare: all Peacock variations are. But this is fabulous. Like you. Grandpa says he remembers the day Uncle Raymond swiped it. He went first wild, then dumb with delight. In fact it was probably that which sent him finally blissfully potty.

SOPHIA Not a bad way to go.

JOHN (*handing it towards her*) So would you like it?

SOPHIA Trying to send me away – or potty?

JOHN Potty.

SOPHIA (*not taking the Peacock*) Suppose you wanted to be an artist but weren't one. You saw, but had no fine co-ordination of hand and eye. Or you had a memory for poetry like music, but couldn't find your own hidden connections between words so as to make them into your own new patterns (or truths). Or you loved people but couldn't understand them. Or you loved God but could never see Him . . . And you came upon this, almost as if you had created it?

JOHN It would be like falling in love.

SOPHIA Except butterflies can't answer you back. (*Walking over to an obvious copy of the Monarch of the Glen - the front of a pile of pictures in the corner*) Can I snoop?

JOHN You already are. I put those there – rescued them from above the old coach house – some damp there slimy as a toadstool. They belonged to Uncle Raymond – sorry, not the butterfly uncle but Grandpa's elder brother killed in the Great War. He was the Adonis of the family. He had the idea of making Bendor – which should have been his – a place people would want to come miles to see. Soon, when Grandpa dies, we shall have no choice but to welcome them whatever we're like! He hadn't much taste, alas. But I love this. Raymond 1, their great grandfather, brought it back from the Peninsular War. Do you like it? Grandpa gave it me for my 21st. Said I'd found it, so I ought to have it. Well, what do you think of it?

SOPHIA I think nothing of it: I know it!

JOHN That's nonsense.

SOPHIA No, you see, it's the same of one of my favourite pictures. In Apsley House, the Water Seller – Velasquez. You see the old man taking from the boy a glass of water. Sort of mutual handing round life, but casually. Who then is thy neighbour? (*Suddenly confused*) It's so wonderful – look at it. But it must be a copy, I suppose.

JOHN You found it, so you should have it.

SOPHIA Don't be silly.

JOHN There might be an occasion when you could refuse me neither that nor anything else.

SOPHIA (*cross*) I could always refuse you that or anything else!

JOHN (*He carries the picture across the Den and props it up on the table against the wall. Then he draws back the curtains*) Look – the strong earth waiting under the snow. That's what I want to give you. (*Points with a sheepish grin at the mistletoe*) Besides it's Christmas.

SOPHIA You don't have to apologise. Or to make excuses.

End Act 1, Scene 2

ACT 1, SCENE 3

(*Christmas Day after lunch, in the Library*)

RORY I hope you don't think we are all like Uncle Richard.

SOPHIA Bored, you mean? He *is* a little too bored to be true.

RORY I didn't think I meant bored. So maybe he is true to himself. Unfortunately.

(*A pause*)

SOPHIA Do you believe in places?

RORY No – nor in faces neither. I am not a painter, like you.

SOPHIA Oh, I am not a painter. But perhaps I do see like one sometimes.

RORY And you like looking.

(*Another pause*)

SOPHIA Watching until it becomes a look. Jeremy at least is normal; and he does things. If I were to paint you – as a group – he would have to be just running in the door to get in the picture at all. The rest I could line up like a late Victorian photograph, a bit faded.

RORY You might paint what we have become, but not how we feel – or at any rate what we feel.

SOPHIA You like making distinctions. (*Again a pause*) You don't belong here, do you? I couldn't fit you into a conversation piece for instance, could I? You don't impinge. Perhaps because you are tall and thin: you'd blow away?

RORY I've been here sixteen years. Why? Difficult to say.

SOPHIA You see? You left Africa. Africa doesn't change: you must have changed.

RORY We say no one changes after the age of seven, or has a new thought after they leave university.

31

SOPHIA You are bored, like the others. As the world turns, do you deserve to survive? Well, I have more snooping to do.

RORY (*smiling faintly*) Settling in?

SOPHIA (*with surprising emphasis*) I shall never settle!

RORY Or take root? Actually I do believe in this place.

SOPHIA So you stayed. (*Shyly*) I think it will not be mine.

RORY Ah! And it was nearly mine too once.

SOPHIA But Africa is bigger.

RORY That doesn't matter. Either you spread ciivilisation in Africa or you preserve it here.

SOPHIA And you chose? Butter spread thin or winter jam from summer fruit? What is Bendor's fruit now?

RORY I didn't choose. There's no choice between equal goods. I found I was not sure of the good. Happy people are engine drivers or photographers from the age of six.

SOPHIA Or earning their daily bread to live. Didn't you ever fall in love.

RORY Now you go and do your snooping somewhere else!

SOPHIA Not here? I wish you could see your face.

RORY So now you can add me to your family snap. (*He stalks out*)

(*Sophia watches him go. Her eyes narrow as she stares at the bookcases, opens each drawer, sits in each chair, then, catching sight of a photograph of John, stands riveted, smiling at herself in the mirror. Enter Madge with tea tray and Jeremy from different directions*)

MADGE (*to Jeremy*) Hey! You'd better grab a cup and scoot or you'll be late for milking.

JEREMY Cows can wait five minutes. They're safe inside and queuing up. I'm beat and they've done nothing but eat all day.

SOPHIA For cows eating is working.

MADGE (*to Sophia*) Didn't you go – the bounds?

JEREMY All right for her. She just floats.

MADGE (*in mocking admonition*) Now, Jeremy!

JEREMY On air, I mean. Of course we didn't swim. That would have finished me. You try a pentathlon with a wood nymph.

MADGE (*to Sophia*) So I gather you enjoyed it. (*To Jeremy*) OK, you take your second cup with you. (*Jeremy exit*)

MADGE (*to Sophia*) But you never thought to help Mrs Hicks with the washing up – why?

SOPHIA (*apologetic*) Sorry. I'm not house-trained.

MADGE You knew there was work to be done. Offer to help and training can begin.

SOPHIA You don't want me here?

33

MADGE Not if you're to turn out like your mother,

SOPHIA (*angrily*) I am not in the least like your sister Alys. If you want to know, that was my resolution in coming here: not to be like her. Why does everyone here look at everyone else here as the image of a parent or an uncle or a grandparent. It's atrocious! I suppose it's because you have never been outside these four walls, so you have no one else to judge by.

MADGE That's rude – even if true.

SOPHIA Well, sorry. I was thinking of something.

MADGE So you left the work to me – like your mother, my sister!

SOPHIA She never thought – on principle. She said you lot spent your time thinking, apparently to make yourselves unhappy. People, she said, have friends and enemies, lovers and children, generally no better than themselves – and some people, if they are unlucky or manage things badly, have to work. She said she couldn't see anything more in it than that, and couldn't see how thinking could help. But I said, that's thinking anyway and sounds wrong. So I keep on thinking. Besides, Alys belonged here, if you do.

MADGE I am not arguing. But if you are here, you help. Please help next time. And at least *I* work.

SOPHIA (*gently but firmly*) Auntie Madge, be gentle with me.

MADGE (*suddenly laughing*) But you have your mother's charm! OK – but you are not made of porcelain, I see that. Alys was; and that was why she could not bear to think – and duly got smashed in the end. Well, now you can learn to wash up while you think, like eating while you talk – but not with your mouth full. You may

34

even find working while you think helps, like music while you work. My Henry said he thought best while shaving, which is why he thought the best leaders are Caesars clean-shaven.

SOPHIA Silly. But they were bald young. I guess they shaved to round it off. Anyway, who was Henry?

MADGE Never you mind. Another member of my family you'll not meet. But even I think sometimes . . .

SOPHIA John says you think so much – of what might have been – that you never talk.

MADGE Damn him for a liar, as I have just proved. But you like him, though. Best thing you can do for him is prove to him he's not porcelain either.

SOPHIA Living in a museum may make you feel either useless or extinct or both. So you work too hard.

MADGE If I didn't know you were showing how clever you are, I'd think you were trying to make up to me.

SOPHIA (*smiling*) From this moment I have decided to dislike you.

(*exit Madge*)

(*Sophia watches Madge go with a sigh of relief and slumps exhausted in Jeremy's chair*)

SOPHIA Golly! I wonder if I'll ever walk again. She at any rate didn't see me shattered . . . Porcelain indeed!

(*She slowly gets up and is staring at a china bowl. She does not move as Robin enters*)

ROBIN You look as though you intend to, *are*, devouring it. Are you taking over the place?

SOPHIA (*looking confused*) Sorry – I was miles away.

ROBIN You looked very much here; and very much at home.

SOPHIA No – I am a waif really.

ROBIN And doing pretty well for yourself here. (*Sophia looks puzzled*) Waif makes good, marries . . .

SOPHIA I see. So that's what you think. Well, I would never marry you, not even to get in from the cold.

ROBIN (*laughing*) I like the calculating ones. It brings them down to my level. They are usually more honest about sex too.

SOPHIA If you think of me like that, you are out of luck.

ROBIN That's not the reason. Careful! You had better be nice to me. Walls have ears. Now last night . . .

SOPHIA (*suddenly no school girl*) I am trying to be patient.

ROBIN Bridling like a duchess. No one will want to believe you. So you just come over here and be good to me. Or else what will the little Bendor dicky-birds be singing . . ?

SOPHIA (*picking up the bowl, slowly walks over towards him*) Cracked and only export ware. Virtually worthless for where it was made – as you are. (*She calmly breaks it over his head*) I enjoyed that. Was it as good for you?

ROBIN Christ! You viper!

SOPHIA Asp actually, with intimations of immortality in mortality. (*She sings lightly, with miming gestures*)
　　Knabe sprach, ich breche dich,
　　Roeslein auf der Heiden;
　　Roeslein sprach, ich steche dich,
　　Dass du ewig denkst an mich –
　　Und ich will's nicht leiden.
　　Roeslein, Roeslein, Roeslein rot, Roeslein auf der Heiden . . .
Schubert à la Goethe, as I trust you know? Boy sings, I pick you; Rose sings, I prick you. I'm just showing you that things as things don't matter. No, even beautiful things. Not even all of this. (*She pivots slowly round with her hands out*) Waifs can go on hungry under the stars.

ROBIN Balls about bigger balls! No matter *that* thing – that the thing wasn't worth money. Last verse: he got her, Clever Clogs, I reckon, in the end. You'll pay for *that*! My head . . .

SOPHIA What end? Luckily it doesn't matter what you think of me. (*She picks up and inspects a shard and drops it again*)

ROBIN Aren't you going to clear it up.

SOPHIA (*laughing*) Certainly not. Your job. You have more to hide here than I have. You tell your tale and I'll tell mine. Even though of course you'll not tell it as it happened. That or any other tale.

ROBIN What is truth? Answer: what people want to believe. You just wait!

SOPHIA My truth is what I believe. But whether or not it is The Truth depends on what I am.

ROBIN I think you are phoney.

SOPHIA But if you're wrong, *you* are!

End Act 1, Scene 3

ACT 1 SCENE 4

(*The family filters into the Dining Room for tea. Robin has still in his hand in a dustpan the China pot fragments after sweeping up, when Richard arrives.*)

ROBIN Sorry, Father, I bumped.

RICHARD Bumptious lad! But it was only China china for European export. Silly Christian fishes.

ROBIN   Ichthys – Jesus Christ Son of God, Saviour.

RICHARD We know. How many times have you told us?

RORY It's His day.

MIRANDA The Queen seemed happy in her address.

RORY So do those two look happy too.

MIRANDA Wouldn't you be?

RORY Might have been.

MIRANDA As I have been. It's sure to be a girl. Easterish, as I am assured today.

RORY Nice change for you. You are sure?

MIRANDA If you don't believe in Providence, you have to believe in the law of averages.

RORY They could be the same thing.

RICHARD God provides the greatest good for the greatest number. So Bendor never is a winner.

MIRANDA For nobody in particular. And we very particular nobodies don't happen to survive in great numbers – even if we do seem to be doing our best at this moment.

SOPHIA What lovely names we give our animals we send extinct - like dodo, moa, quagga, great auk. Bendor sounds lovely.

RICHARD Homo insipiens.

JEREMY We are shut in like a game park. There's snow on the ground and soft rain now on the windows; and we stare at our reflection.

ROBIN Cold and wet only go to make us roast peasant.

MIRANDA Caliban! So, Jeremy, we must take our chances.

ROBIN If you have them.

RICHARD You must take them!

RORY Not at someone else's expense.

MIRANDA Every vigorous man takes the light off someone else.

RORY Some live better in the shade.

MIRANDA (*kindly*) Or in the Seminary?

RORY I am still happier here.

MIRANDA At Christmas we are even more shut in!

RORY Bendor makes no artificial demands on me.

RICHARD So make no artificial demands on yourself. You should have stayed in the Seminary. (*exit*)

MIRANDA And yet you run the estate when Richard would like to. Why?

RORY Another second best.

(*Rory and Miranda sit smiling into the fire*)

RORY Well, Jeremy – are the bounds well beaten?

JEREMY Sophe said she was tired before we went – and ran me into the ground. Must flush out the dairy. (*exit*)

ROBIN I quite see!

MADGE (*still watching TV and hissing*) Shush!

Robin (*carefully also hissing, intentionally like a snake*) Sorry. (*After a pause*) A nasty permissive film this. On Christmas Day, too. Tut-tut!

SOPHIA If you don't like it, why watch?

ROBIN I see the little maiden likes it. Not like you?

MADGE Run along, Robin.

(*Enter John, who firmly takes Sophia's hand into the Library*)

ROBIN (*louder and following them into the Library*) John – aren't you two afraid of ghosts? Last night . . .

RICHARD (*also following with the others*) John, you do look as though you've seen one.

ROBIN I heard noises – and voices – last night; and I'm sure they came from your wing, John.

RICHARD Voices?

ROBIN A man's and a woman's – a girl's rather – yes, and noises. Loud noises well after midnight. Sort of splashing and bumps.

RORY (*to Miranda*) Our ghosts?

RICHARD (*to John*) Didn't you hear them? (*silence*) Answer me, John! (*drawing himself up*) John, Sophia – does this mean what I am afraid it must mean. (*silence. Then to Robin*) Does it?

(*Rory and Miranda hurriedly disappear*)

ROBIN I fear so.

MADGE (*also leaving*) Richard, be very careful!

RICHARD So this is how you use your new-subsidised independence? Sweet seventeen, Sophia – just. And your own first cousin.

JOHN Father, I . . .

RICHARD You don't deny Sophia was in what you are pleased to call your Den around midnight?

JOHN No.

RICHARD Your bathroom.

JOHN No.

RICHARD Your bedroom?

JOHN In fact, yes! Denied!

RICHARD I can't throw you right out of Bendor now unfortunately. Not quite. But get out of here! (*But John stays*)

(*Enter Grandfather who has been hanging in the Library doorway*)

GRANDFATHER John, you have let me down.

John Yes.

GRANDFATHER John, you have let yourself down.

JOHN No.

GRANDFATHER Do you know, I believe you. But from now on you are on your own. (*exeunt John and` Sophia. Almost at once Richard follows, re-appears in the Dining Room, his pretence of anger immediately evaporating*)

GRANDFATHER (*now from the Library speaking to Richard across the divide into the Dining Room*) Would you like us to audition?

RICHARD (*shortly*) I'm not with you.

GRANDFATHER You have made Bendor a set for your amateur theatricals; and I was wondering what you are putting on for us next? Yesterday you set a trap – for me, I guess – which you fell into yourself, and then tried to cover up by a nasty attack on Miranda. Today you spoil things for John and Sophia; and your absurd public attitudinising makes it unnecessary even to find out – preferably in private – what in fact went on. So I just wanted you to show me what part I am supposed to play?

RICHARD Do you still have a part – and do you think it matters exactly what went on? Is it not my business, as Sophia's guardian, to know it was wrong?

GRANDFATHER Not necessarily – and depending on your motive to inquire. John's and Sophia's love is in the mould. Every look, every word, affects it. What matters most is, that they with reverence treat each other and we their love. And I suspect that what we do is more likely to hurt them than anything they are likely to do among themselves. If you want to watch anyone, how about you watch your dear Robin with May? She is a warm-hearted creature, and he must look to her very brilliant and high. Hardly an even contest. Besides, he's an attractive so-and-so.

RICHARD Then yes, I have a part for you. How about you leave off playing heavy father, and try instead heavy grandfather?

GRANDFATHER (*suddenly quiet and a bit foxy*) Are you afraid of taking off your make-up?

RICHARD So as to play your game? What's your mask? You have always looked too good to be true.

GRANDFATHER I guess I am too old to know, let alone take it off. It's what I've become – not pretending like you to be bad, but pretending to be good.

RICHARD Dishonest then of you now, stooping like Jove pretending to be human, so as to seduce me.

GRANDFATHER Aren't you afraid you might become bad? Suppose you found you had become too old to take off your make-up. Suppose yours was no longer a snake's skin to slough. Your life would be no longer a game, let alone a joke. And therefore of course it would no longer amuse you.

RICHARD Did you enjoy pretending to be good? And now being good?

GRANDFATHER Not so much. I do enjoy being. And you are right, the state of my soul does not titillate me. But I hate the hurt of seeing my family louse themselves up out of nowhere.

RICHARD (*laughing*) I confess I still enjoy being bad. So I suppose that according to you I am not beyond redemption.

GRANDFATHER You may well be beyond redemption. Neither of us is your judge – nor indeed mine. And I agree if by now I am not redeemed I probably never shall be. But I am talking about whether you are vulnerable. You have wronged me; you are tearing my house apart. You have wronged Miranda and Rory, Sophia and John. You have ruined Robin most, by flattery – your ape faceless in your mirror. Suppose we turned on you.

RICHARD I am stronger than all of them. I am stronger even than you, because I am younger. And if you are all nasty to me, I can always disarm you by turning nice.

GRANDFATHER You are vulnerable then because you are separable from your mask. Therefore you are not immune to guilt – guilt which tears, even when it cannot restore. You believe in ghosts, you say. And Bendor air can be very heavy.

End Act 1, Scene 4

ACT 1, SCENE 5

(Boxing Day. The Den. John is staring out of the bow window. Enter Rory.)

JOHN Morning, sahib. It's thawing.

RORY *(shyly)* I have come to lecture you on morals.

JOHN You know I always listen to you – if you are speaking for yourself.

RORY Sophia – she is very young.

JOHN *(laughing)* Not too young to know what she wants!

RORY Perhaps she is just impressionable and you have impressed her.

JOHN A very particular kind of impression: she loves me. She has made the same impression on me. Why is love better called by another name?

RORY Love is final as death.

JOHN I don't know what happens after love.

RORY You go on living – but with a different mind.

JOHN Not with another body? No Resurrection? Or if you are lucky, a man sharing his girl's body and mind. Extra eyes, nose, touch, ears . . . *(grinning)* Even using an extra body, for some purposes.

RORY But if you aren't lucky, only with an extra body with perhaps an inversion or even perversion of your own mind. Sooner or later the mirror cracks and you can't even see yourself.

JOHN Oh do let's stop playing Hamlet and Polonius. Anyone can define the distinction between love and infatuation. Moral rules even are generally agreed. The difficulties arise in applying the rules to situations that different people see differently. I say I love Sophia and she loves me. You say either or both of us is infatuated. So let's start there.

RORY I say only that you may be – and that time not intensity of feeling is the test.

JOHN We are both under fire you know.

RORY Yes, I have lowered my shield to throw my spear.

JOHN Are or were you in love with Mother?

RORY I don't know.

JOHN How much more time will tell – and what will you do about it?

RORY I don't know when – or in fact what then.

JOHN If when you die you still think you may be, you'll assume you always were?

RORY Damn!

JOHN The fact is now, because of Father you'll always be at arm's length. Before time can start to run, you have to get right in there. Do you think now you were right to leave the Mission?

RORY (*uneasily*) I lost my Faith. (*hesitates*) Your mother was only a symptom of the disease. I didn't know that then.

JOHN Golly – only a symptom. Then you certainly weren't in love – if that's how you now think of it! Poor old Mum! But she made the right choice. Even Pa must have been better than that. But if that's so, how do you know that you lost your Faith? Shouldn't you feel that you had seen the darkness at last? I am not being impertinent, I hope. Nor, certainly, just making debating points: I just want to know what Faith is – or now what you think Faith is, which seems not at all necessarily the same thing. What is Faith – and how do you know whether you have it or not?

RORY If I had more sense, I'd creep behind a smoke screen of wounded feelings. I hate losing arguments.

JOHN (*laughing*) Crying touché is only another way of disappearing. I suppose I am asking whether love, to be love – or Faith, to be Faith – must have two constituents, a feeling and a habit? Does it take time for the second to grow, by which time you are telling me, if the first has gone, it's too late for love (or Faith) to repair it? In which case no falling in love can either be love or be certain to result in it. And no Faith a living Faith.

RORY Some day, some time, a moment of decision comes. In a sense you don't have to decide: the decision is there. As a Jesuit, you follow routine, a mind-breaking routine of prayer and action, prayer and action. Your duty is to find God and to define how to treat your neighbour. Often you feel ill-at-ease. Especially if for a moment you haven't too much to do – like an engine revving out of gear. Or you fuss about your soul when really you have been praying badly or shirked writing a letter. So the habit comes as the feeling goes. The habit replaces the feeling, but only by degrees. And so for a while you live on the habit and forbear to look for the feeling. You call it selfish and egotistical even to ask for the feeling. But you do ask. For if you don't ask you are no longer a churchman. You have become perhaps a social administrator or a diplomat or even just a politicking busybody. But either way, asking or not, the voice never comes. You are a crab's shell, wearing the habit with no feeling. I lost my Faith. I knew I was alone.

JOHN Then why not kill yourself? I couldn't bear that loneliness, not to hope – especially if I had failed.
   Hell? God lost lost dog.
  Heaven? Love secured. Purgatory?
   Hell in His company.

RORY Dilemma: cowardly to do it and cowardly not.

JOHN So you considered it – topping yourself?

RORY Probably. But if I was right there'd be no point; and if I was wrong, I'd look rather silly – and ungrateful – on the other side. Like Hamlet. But just like the dramatist, I never could make the leap direct out of tragedy (that is the darkness comprehended, as St John might say) into comedy. The Bard seems in unbridgeable disconnect.

JOHN Shakespeare was a recusant. But Luther was right: the Church grows out of conscience and must not, because it cannot, replace it. No indulgences please!

RORY For what you were doing last night?

JOHN So I don't think my feelings will change that quickly! You're sure love and Faith are the same – or to be treated the same?

RORY Faith and love are journeys with sign posts. I got the sequence wrong and got lost.

JOHN Cradle Catholic never climbs out of cradle into divine comedy?

RORY Grown up joy only grows out of pain. Otherwise pain and loss or whatever's dreadful are unendurable, so unintelligible.

JOHN Love can be so damnably painful.

RORY Not even Shakespeare could grow Twelfth Night out of Lear. Comedy grows out of tragedy endured and understood. So King Lear is unintelligible – as Shakespeare's Fool.

JOHN So – the play is unendurable? And king unendurably alone . . . So you lost your Catholic Faith to become a Prot? Erasmus did that rather better. I'm sorry he then refused to be made a cardinal!

RORY I am your bad beginner-Prot, I fear. But just so I hope to grow up into comedy. (recites)

Purgatory-In-Waiting
The toils in arabesque through time of Fate's narration
    The Bard inscrutinises: his Purgatory
    From Here to There, in moral tragedy
And pain beyond bearing, binds no truth's sure seen relation

    To Faith's conversion, immersed in confluence
Of firmament secure with conscience, that still we seek.
Transfigure to unity universes but words we speak,
    Not persons: the pneumosphere is Here. No sense

In pilgrim's freedoms else. All treasure's in expectation
    Unearthed of doubt. No Church grafts yet Faith's Tree
    To plant out 'his' or 'hers', as their oblation. Hence –
Faith grows *what* conscience light from primal dark and bleak?

JOHN Of course if you just wait for Godot, he never comes. You knew that well enough. Here, Uncle, is another douzet: you wrote it for poor Mother; and she made me read it her, in the hope I might explain it. I did try.

Theodicy The Odyssey

Word starts from dark, on rhythm runs, to end in rhyme:
  In petty pace the universe sublime.
  The snatch beyond need of others' needs is crime.
Theodicy hangs the pendulum of dancing time

  Long fated: fun fêted in pomp are joys that mime
Love's simple truth: in births all equal respected prime
One ecosystem, diseased man's will spoiled Gaia's clime;
  Cruel Nature teaches the wisdom worth a dime:

Her gifts unmined, mind's empathy, from primal slime
  To robot tech forge Odyssey divine.
  No young face brighter shines than washed of grime.
From tragedy's dark to comic light of Faith, the climb!

    Moment's conversion:
   In purgatory together
   Know heaven in hell.

Your great friend de Chardin's 'pneumosphere' implied
humanity's evolving a sort of universal empathy, with everybody
intercommunicating lovingly with everyone else. But that
unlovingly must become an autistic nightmare, a cacophony of
meaningless unfriendly chatter, until unified by some overwhelming
Spirit of love, however pervasive e.g. electronic communications.

RORY Teilhard – oh, he was a prophet of divine science! He saw the
Universe growing to One Te Deum, Jubilate, Benedicite.

JOHN 'All ye works of the Lord, praise ye the Lord!'

RORY His hymn of the universe: 'The wonder of His works
displays the firmament!' (Haydn.)

JOHN (*sings a fragment ofHaydn's Creation chorus*) . . . 'Displays the firmament, displays the firmament!' 'Fire, fire!' (Pascal) 'Rage, rage against the dying of the light!' (Dylan Thomas) 'Io Paean! Hymen, hymenaee!' (Delphi & Epidaurus) . . . By the way, where is Sophia? Do you know? It's a bit strange. For I've been expecting her a while . . . But that's not the way our world turns – not yet anyhow.

RORY So you must trundle dogged on.

JOHN Buggering on, so Winnie said . . . As flying ants fallen, like Icarus?

Why, Icarus, O my Crusader – with what idea
    Take flight? You saw the sky as lightning strike!
    I snapped one August night, as nothing like,
Those battlements by lightning light. My atmosphere,

    Not castle, burnt. Love's seizure of the heart
For Ganymede was Faith. So ordinary world for me
Was made a wonder by my girl extraordinary:
    No sculpted Faith of mine, no art could start

Such transport for fallen flying ant, though flightless, drear.
    For stony – though Love and Faith are One – the hike,
    And humdrum the pilgrimage where we are but part –
But patterned by Creation's background memory.

    Prot and Catholic can't live side by side,
    Not seeing themselves groom and bride.
      For his conscience, her root,
      From which she sprouts their shoot:
    They split Christ with their marriage denied.

So you suffer like a tragic hero, as if you are in love (or as if with a vocation?) Then somehow sometime, a joyous – comic? – decision.

51

That cannot be: I think rather you must express your love in your habit of living, until your heart is lightened to light, whatever happens? Or may there come a moment, Uncle, when you must force the pace?

RORY I am not so sure of that.

JOHN Should that not be the essential judgment: when to turn thought into action?

RORY Perhaps – but certainly no one is this priest who wins his Faith or falls in love overnight.

JOHN So is Faith always a battle? And I am engaged to Sophia but not married to her?

RORY So leave her alone and intact for a bit?

JOHN (*cross*) But I did leave her 'alone and intact' as you put it . . . Where is she by the way? This is strange. I was expecting her.

RORY Good for you. But I don't write morals in inverted commas. You have made her a promise: can you keep it?

JOHN If the family will leave us alone!

RORY (*obviously hurt*) I didn't want to interfere, only to help.

JOHN I'm sorry. It slipped out. What should I do?

RORY Let the conflagration die out, if it's going to. Wait – not long necessarily. Say six months, or just even until Easter. You owe that to Sophia.

(*Lights down for one full minute*)

JEREMY (*calling from off-stage*) John, Sophia's gone! You've missed her. (*Jeremy bursts in onto an empty stage*) Where are you? Here, she gave me this for you. (*Jeremy leaves John on an easel a sketch of two heads, John's and Sophia's. Lights briefly down again. Re-enter John, looking angry, with Rory*)

JOHN You knew she was going, even while we were talking? All that religious stuff was just to divert and detain me? So I couldn't even say good-bye to Sophia! Father knows you vacillate, so he uses you to hold me back from what he knows, even if you don't, that I should want to do! Or were you jealous too?

RORY Yes. I'm sorry, I suppose. But all I said I do believe is true.

JOHN True is true, whoever says it. But who knows what's told them is true, if it's told to deceive?

End Act 1, Scene 5

ACT 1, SCENE 6

(*John and Sophia in night clothes – chiming diaries in separate pools of light, surrounds invisible*)

JOHN Boxing Day 11pm. Mother has sent Sophia away. Because of last night.

SOPHIA From Christmas Dayto the midnight after. So I am out of John's Bendor because Uncle Richard says so.

JOHN But what do they know (or care) about Christmas Night?

SOPHIA But what do they know about our Christmas? How crude they are – like that horrible word intercourse, that sounds like a confluence of sewers! As if food were only calories.

53

JOHN Dear Robin hears a splashin' and a squeakin' and a gigglin'. So – because they are all jealous we are immediately classed as miscreants and a shame on the Family. As if loving were miscreation.

SOPHIA As if the lightest kisses don't always taste best: most anyway mightn't even be better than a perfect orgy on a bed. Well, for a young maiden anyway? So I'll tell you (*She curtsies to her diary*) what did happen, if you like. Remember the rules – and no scratching out. Truth is indelible. (*She curtsies again*)

JOHN She runs out again and I think I have seen the last of her – as I might well have done! But she is back in an instant with an easel and a huge sketching pad: why, she says, don't we sketch each other? 'Passing life on' – odd phrase.

SOPHIA Truth, which is immortality.

JOHN After a while I say I can't see her in the snow light. It's a clear night; but the moon, naturally, is at the side of the house. So I say, why don't we give ourselves a clearer outline? And I don't mean, turn on the light or even put on another log. A complete outline. She looks hard at me; but she does it. So do I. Still we can't see much – least of all the paper.

SOPHIA You'll say I should not have suggested it; and John was naughty too. But boys will be men and girls . . ? I wanted something tangible, something made on our first night – not that I was thinking like that of our 'first night' – not then anyway. 'Excuses'? Yes – and anyway it didn't work. When it was my turn to sketch I could see just how little John had seen of me – and that my eyes are no better than his. I turned round and he joined me in the window. Now we could see. I sometimes feel that bay windows are outside. These became wings bearing us along silver sinuations out to sea. And the sea was light; and it drained our blood until we were light too.

JOHN When Sophia suggests a bathe I know what she means. But I pretend to take her at her word. Only . . .

SOPHIA And there was nothing to be afraid of. And we went slowly through his bedroom to the bathroom. As the bath ran we passed the time, shall we say? Then he picked me up and flung me in and jumped in after.

JOHN Only it's a cold bath. You try the sea at Christmas! At first my dear Sophia doesn't see the joke. But the right joke always completes the best comedy. Timing is logic.

SOPHIA A cold bath! And just when I am ready to . . . Hm . . . Even the Rule does not require me to set down in stone bare possibilities. But some day . . . He'd better watch out! You'll see. (*She curtsies again*)

(*The lights fade a moment and come up again*)

JOHN February 14th – Valentine's, not a good day. I should have gone or at any rate written. It's term time; and 'time tryeth troth'. But six or seven weeks and not to send a word? Silly that she should be at school, when there is so much here we could teach each other. And silly to wait when I anyway have no doubt!

SOPHIA 'Yes?' Scratch that out. 'No.' Scratch that out. So I cannot curtsey to you now. 'Perhaps?' Scratch that out. Write nothing. *Nothing!*

JOHN Or was it all too slick? Too easy?

SOPHIA No, that's cowardly. And no scratching out. But I shall not curtsey to you now. I kneel. The truth is Yes. It was natural for both of us. So it must be right.

JOHN I know what I feel now: how do I know how I shall feel? But who ever knows that? I should have gone today to her, at least.

SOPHIA But I cannot excuse the silence: artificial, so superficial.

JOHN Stick it out, as I promised – if I did? – till Easter. But remember or be damned: never again take advice, so as to evade decision.

SOPHIA My John superficial? You have caught me, dear pen, in a doubt. (*smiles*) So that's why I wanted to say nothing to you? But say to him, nothing. Faith requires: if he is silent, I am silent.

JOHN If I cannot trust my own judgement, what right – or capacity – have I to trust some one else's?

SOPHIA Perhaps Uncle Richard had John's letters intercepted. He is mean enough.

JOHN Not writing was unforgivable.

SOPHIA All right then – challenge Mother Ann! She'd know and she'd not lie. No, you're right. I don't believe it.

JOHN Please God, let her forgive me!

(*His light goes out*)

SOPHIA (*looking out of a window*} Stream on, stars. They are nearer than he is. Their light older than glaciers. But they talk. Worse than the pain, being dammed from the stream of things. From ooze, lizard and ape, even to Alys and Sophia and *stop*! John swirled me away in a minute waltz, then cast me up as another of nature's wrecks . . . Stream on, Easter . . . So Mother Ann said. The suspense (*she chuckles*) is killin' me. One look will be enough to damn or bless him. Hell – that pain again! If I let on to Mother Ann, she'll send me back, like a sick child – their child. I shall not give them that satisfaction!

(*Her light goes out*)

End Act 1

INTERVAL

ACT 2, SCENE 1

(*Rory and Miranda: the Dining Room, Good Friday morning*)

MIRANDA Easter should always be as late as this, the egg almost hatched. Earlier, spring is a promise that may be taken back.

RORY I don't think Good Friday belongs to spring at all.

MIRANDA For you nowadays Good Friday doesn't belong to Easter.

RORY Nor Easter to you.

MIRANDA Your fault.

RORY How mine?

MIRANDA I believed in Easter because you did. For you Easter seemed possible. I look angelic; but I am irredeemably earthy, and muddy at that. Earth watered down. But I am also lazy and needed a star, to keep me awake; so I admired you. I was very Catholic. But you were never what I wanted to be. Nor what I wanted.

RORY So I was your little airy fairy. Thank heaven you never came out with this before. So why now?

MIRANDA Doesn't spring (even if not Easter) make you think of Sophia?

RORY And John?

MIRANDA Yes. Well?

RORY I should say we are quits. I killed Easter for you; and you killed romance for me.

MIRANDA Charming.

RORY We both deserved it.

MIRANDA Who set you in judgment over me? As judge in your own cause?

RORY (*suddenly gentle*) Our cause, same cause. Faith and love. We are alike as two peas. Each pea has two halves, but our difference is that we are not ashamed of our same halves.

MIRANDA It would never have worked. I could never have loved what I admired. And you could never have been the man I could have loved.

RORY A woman can love practically any thing; but once she has loved she can't love another thing. If she does, it's only to alter it. Didn't you try to alter me?

MIRANDA I admired you; and I thought you could manage your inheritance at least as well as Richard had, in your place. I was sorry for you. I didn't want you.

RORY I knew that. I am wrong to try to blame you.

MIRANDA Better blame me than despair of yourself! When you relinquished your profession you made yourself professionally unhappy. Fifteen years of it. Managing the estate for Richard, which he would much rather have gone on doing himself, till finally your father saw neither of you would ever do anything with it, and gave it to John instead. Once a priest always a priest. You still think like one, don't you?

RORY Do you know for the first time in my life, I admire you? Any moment now, I'll see I never loved you.

MIRANDA You knew that too. Do you know, today is the first time that you have ever mentioned me and love in the same breath? And now you have rejected the connection.

RORY Why didn't we talk like this before – long before?

MIRANDA Because there was nothing we wanted more than our fantasies. Now there is?

RORY Now there is?

MIRANDA Yes! John and Sophia. John with Sophia. What are we going to do? Is she going, after all the other girls have gone home, to stay in that damned prison on Sunday? Where else can she go but here? But I suppose we are still to keep up the ridiculous pretence that she is a leper to corrupt the Virgin Bendor – or more particularly John? I love John; and I love Sophia. And I love John-and-Sophia.

RORY Yes!

(*Enter unannounced Mother Ann*)

MOTHER ANN Mrs St Columba, may I speak to you alone, please?

MIRANDA But of course, Mother. I'm sorry (*in a tone suggesting she is not*), but I was not expecting you.

MOTHER ANN Quite so. (*A pointed look at Rory, who leaves hurriedly and looking worried*) I asked to see you alone because I am used to dealing with women.

MIRANDA (*with an uneasy smile*) But not to visiting parents on Good Friday after end of term: Sophia?

MOTHER ANN I don't trust the telephone – that is, myself over the telephone. I learn as much in an expression as in a voice; and that is how I would like people to come to know me.

MIRANDA Yes of course.

MOTHER ANN We nuns are not disembodied spirits.

Miranda (*impatient*) Please let me have your news.

MOTHER ANN Sophia had appendicitis.

MIRANDA Had? If it is over . . .

MOTHER ANN (*more gently*) Yes, it is over. We at the school had no warning. Girls in their last year have their own rooms. When the maid called her because she had not appeared in school, she could see that Sophia was very ill, though Sophia denied it. I was told, though – and sent her straight to the hospital A & E. But she was dead on arrival.

MIRANDA In three months I heard nothing of her pains or her agonies from her. None of us did, except perhaps John? That I do not know. And I am ashamed that I found the surprising silence a relief.

MOTHER ANN I too found her a puzzle – until now. We were long used to having her for part of the holidays, so it now excited no comment, even from Christmas, among the few other girls we had with us. And when term started, she seemed her old self. It took an experienced eye to detect strain, though naturally I remembered what you had told me. Nevertheless her work if anything was even better than ever. Some of her drawings too quite excited Miss Stubbins; and Sister Aloysia kept coming to me saying she had found some one who could think in Greek. I had already of course spoken to Sophia about an Oxbridge scholarship. But please forgive me speaking (and thinking) like a school mistress.

MIRANDA But please go on. Remember, you have been more of a mother to her than I have.

MOTHER ANN (*looking hard at her old pupil*) Yes – that I think is true, Very well. As I was saying, Sophia gave us no trouble. There were no unseemly huddles with other girls. She did not use her exciting experience to win their dubious admiration. And I am sure – maybe unfortunately – that she had no confidante. As for myself, I had been expecting dumb insolence: Sophia is a headstrong girl.

MIRANDA (*almost under her breath*) Was!

MOTHER ANN (*put out by her slip but firmly continuing*) But she never avoided my eye or caught it unnecessarily. Instead her manners could not have been more charming; and she succeeded in making me feel that here was a young woman out of place in my school. It is unusual for my girls – (*grimly*) whatever their experiences – to achieve such self-possession before they leave. But all the time I was suspicious. For all the time I was sure this aloofness was just a sophisticated version of the secretiveness I had been expecting.

MIRANDA She must have been in constant pain.

MOTHER ANN Sustained discomfort at least – and, yes, I am sure, occasionally in great pain. But she never said anything. Somehow, she never even looked pale, as if with a heavy period. I never saw her wince. I was watching her like a hawk; and she outwitted me. (*getting up, with Miranda following suit*) I am glad I didn't know what she must have been thinking of me, her blind captor. For I was very fond of her . . . But I shouldn't have such selfish thoughts, much less give expression to them.

MIRANDA Mother, thank you. I have known you many years. It is still a help – as well you know! – to know that at St Clare's Sophia was . . . in kindly hands; and she will have liked a worthy adversary. I wonder . . . She looked on the pain as if her own body was voicing her misery?

MOTHER ANN It probably was.

MIRANDA Sophia must have been . . . very lonely.

MOTHER ANN I usually know when my girls are receiving letters. I do not think Sophia received any.

MIRANDA And, to our shame, no visitors.

MOTHER ANN But I do have a letter for John that she left for him. It was on her desk. I think he should have it.

MIRANDA (*sinks suddenly back into her chair, then recollects herself*) Oh, do forgive me. You too have been standing all this time.

MOTHER ANN (*sits down again, pleased*) I have not forgotten you too were once my pupil, even if I have not seen you anywhere in my world since your wedding. Till now you have been as a stranger.

MIRANDA I'm afraid I have lost touch with a lot of good people. (*a pause*) And good things.

MOTHER ANN In which category do you place your God now?

MIRANDA (*laughing*) I see you have not forgotten me. But, thank you, I have not made a God out of Bendor. Not like some others. Maybe I have lost contact with Bendor too!

MOTHER ANN So Bendor has rejected you also. Has Bendor a soul?

MIRANDA Bendor is a broad and peaceful place.

MOTHER ANN The grave's a fine and private place?

MIRANDA (*laughing again*) The grave too must have some kindly space. But we – even you nuns? – make everything we are fond of – children, house, (*with a cheeky grin*) vocation? – into images of our struggles. We all love Bendor. But their images are not mine. But that's marriage – save that I didn't fight.

MOTHER ANN A house divided: perhaps they feel the same. I hope from now you will have another chance to help them, in part at least, to superimpose? Never too late to mend. Don't think I didn't notice: carriage shows long before clothes. Perhaps if it's a girl you'll call her Sophia and I can be godmother? A second chance for me too maybe. I shall not again apologise for selfish thoughts. Besides I'd like an excuse to come back here sometimes.

MIRANDA Yes, Mother.

MOTHER ANN No don't move. I showed myself in; I can show myself out. As Sophia did. (*exit*)

(*Miranda moves slowly over to a small writing desk in the corner. A pause, then she reads out from what she has written*)

63

MIRANDA I am at the bay window giving on to the Saxon Oak in the sunset. The evening is perfectly clear and still. The finest memories are of evanescent things. How stilted that sounds: but I am trying to find an excuse for not ending this letter, as if today and Sophia have not quite gone until I write the last word. With my love, your helpless Mama.

End Act 2, Scene 1

ACT 2, SCENE 2

(*The Den*)

JOHN (*reading*) 'My very dear son, I have dreadful news for you, of which you can have had no warning. Sophia died this morning of appendicitis. The end at least was quick. I am at the bay window giving on to the Saxon oak in the sunset . . .' (*A pause*) She is not my ship, the hollow oak, her rigging gone, only her hull sprouting shoots, in a round fuzz like barnacles. Not my tree, not my mother, not my father. 'From now on you walk alone.' I wonder, will theirs be a girl?

RORY (*enters diffidently*) May I come in?

JOHN (*waving letter*) Dreadful being a priest after the event. Mama couldn't face me – sent this. So Jeremy . . . had to tell me first. (*Sees letter in Rory's hand*) Oh, no – not another letter! Oh, I see, from Sophia. This time her writing is like a frenzied ant. Most unlike her. And she returns the Black Peacock? Give it me and read!

RORY Must I? Now? Very well. (*Reads*) 'John, you were dear once. But you never wrote. I have been ill but hardly noticed. When I wanted you, you were not here. I do not want you now. Your Sophia.'

64

JOHN (*Moves to the bay window in a reverie*)
Consider a garden: nothing more English or
Well-tempered. Nature groomed vigorous,
Wisteria curls after jostling daffodils
In extravagant hats. In miniature soon
The leaf on ash like Baby's fingers.
Rooks already in rush hour, rolling like tipsy bees.
Oh, to breathe the springy airs again in balance!
In all the million aeons that ride from here
To time reversed, there is no fitter place
For God to walk. But in continuum
There are no stopping places.

Sophia had an exquisite sense of time and timing.

RORY Suppose she was an actress and knew what you are in for too. Don't believe she meant it.

JOHN She did and she didn't; so she has left me a choice what and how to believe. Yet that was not what I'd call an ambiguous letter. She was setting the record straight . . .

RORY And resetting the stop watch? You start again.

JOHN She didn't soften the blow. Don't you! Truth is for novelists. I must simplify. (*Seeing Rory hurt*) How pompous – damn! I'm sorry.

RORY Decisiveness is fine if there's something to be done.

JOHN Oh, yes – I have time. But the stopwatch has already been running. No good just staring at it. Or is that always your way?

RORY I didn't mean you to turn your searchlight on me.

JOHN If in the darkness, a sentry like Hamlet on the battlements, you stare at the most chaotic shape from many points, you'll see for sure a pattern. Hence the kaleidoscope. The hero's presiding over his own destruction? Or his family's? Or God's? Or chaos manipulated by a confused and reluctant brain after the event? For then the pattern is always irrelevant to action.

RORY You ask so many questions, you cannot want the answers; so you will always be wrong.

JOHN One thing, Uncle, I do know. If you don't look, you will never regain your Faith.

RORY For that I retain my conscience. What more than that does Mr Know-All inform me I need?

JOHN (*makes a despairing gesture as Rory leaves in a huff*) Oh, John, look where inactivity has got you. Trying to do 'the right thing'. You're as old as he is before his time.

RICHARD (*entering and eyeing Miranda's letter*) I see you've heard the news.

JOHN Yes.

RICHARD I'm sorry. A bad business.

JOHN Why did you do it – sending her away?

RICHARD I'm afraid I was a bit hasty.

JOHN To do what?

RICHARD Don't be silly. It was my job to look after Sophia – protect her.

JOHN What were you protecting her from?

RICHARD This isn't the time to go into all that. It's all over.

JOHN Blimey! You think that? Not for me. And the past is not erased because somebody dies. Besides, you never went into it then.

RICHARD I don't recollect you pressing me. And I don't hold with post-mortems. (*John winces so sharply that even Richard notices*) But *much more gently*) you should let it rest. You must let Sophia rest.

JOHN But, Father, there is a mystery.

RICHARD Accidents are always caused? Nonsense: she had appendicitis – and probably from a burst, therefore peritonitis. No mystery in that. Every year thousands die of it.

JOHN Nowadays for undiagnosed appendicitis there's always some one to blame: doctors, parents, the patients themselves. For example, she must have had a great deal of pain beforehand. But for some reason no one heard about it. I need to get behind the physical fact. We made Sophia our victim. But what were we meaning to achieve by sending her away and leaving her to die alone?

RICHARD What utter self-serving nonsense! Sophia was as fit as a yearling when she left Bendor. (*He looks pleased at his simile, then checks himself.*) The fact is, you are trying to turn a very ordinary misfortune into high tragedy. Presumably you hope that will make it easier for you to bear, fossilising the event to suspend it out of context. But in the convent she was in good hands. And she was a very grown-up seventeen anyway. If anyone left Sophia to die, it is you!

JOHN (*with a grin of pain, and for the first time allowing an edge into his voice*) Precisely: she was seventeen and grown up, as you say. So why did you do it? What were you protecting her from? From me? From herself? Please help me to understand.

RICHARD You understand well enough. You had misbehaved in my . . . in your grandfather's house.

JOHN If 'misbehaved' is a euphemism, we didn't. Not that you made that your concern to find out. If you had cared, why did you not ask? I shouldn't have lied. It was something between us, so why should I try to fool you? As it was, it was enough for your convenience that Robin had put us in a 'compromising position'. And position wasn't the word either.

RICHARD One thing leads to another. I see I sent Sophia away just in time.

JOHN Just in time for what? How could you know without enquiring where 'things' were leading us? But in fact did you doubt that we were hoping to get married?

RICHARD No – but we all of us thought you should both have time to think things over coolly before you got too entangled. Besides – wasn't it all just a bit too slick, and more than a little incestuous really? With your first cousin? One evening you get an estate; and that night you get a girl. You have neither of you flown the nest; and it's even the same nest! Marriage is not like that. And no woman is content in the long run with a milksop.

JOHN (*openly angry*) You weren't concerned with her happiness or mine. You were merely angry and jealous that Grandpa gave Bendor estate to me, not to you. One evening you don't get an estate, and next day . . .

RICHARD Don't you cheek me, my little man! If you had had the guts of a rabbit, you'd have gone to see her. Then you'd have seen soon enough what state she was in, how ill she was, and set her straight. Or at the very meanest least you'd have written. A fine passionate Romeo you were! All this cross-examination of your father, which I only put up with out consideration for your feelings, has been an elaborate but crude attempt at self-justification. I was right, even Robin was right. You were never the man to run Bendor. You weren't even in love!

JOHN 'I am sorry. A bad business.' (*A pause*) It must be dreadful to be like you. You are a mean cad and unworthy of Bendor. Will you please go? Now!

RICHARD Damned if I do! (*But he goes*)

(*John follows Richard out of the Den and reappears in the Dining Room*)

JOHN (*to himself*) You were right, though – a milksop! a vacillator, a Rory, a Hamlet! There is no glory in wanting to do the right thing. It only encourages dictators.

GRANDFATHER (*standing in Library speaks across the divide into the Dining Room*) Not a nice sentiment.

JOHN (*defiant rather than embarrassed*) It's not just him. He's phoney anyhow. But I suppose I was a bit silly, since that was just what Father wanted.

GRANDFATHER So who are the other dictators?

JOHN (*evasive for once*) Anyone who sees my life as a mere extension of theirs.

GRANDFATHER That's very selfish.

69

JOHN I can't speak for myself. I have no feelings, only my head left. Bendor has dismembered me.

Grandfather 'Love with no strings attached is what I want,' said the puppet.

JOHN I could not have put it more brutally myself. Thank you, Grandpa.

GRANDFATHER Disinterested love is not human. We identify with whom and what we love. It's the only compliment that counts or determines action.

JOHN Then how is it that only Sophia and I suffer?

GRANDFATHER Not so; and if it appears so, it is only our incompetence. It would be grossly unfair for example to tie round Uncle Rory's neck the label you have just now hung around your father's.

JOHN Or around your neck, Grandpa? And must I be just? Why, wronged, can't I just be angry?

GRANDFATHER You can't, if I'm to take seriously what your talking head says!

JOHN But the truth can be more cruel than abuse. You'll probably agree that Uncle Rory was carefully inveigled by my dear Papa into taking Uncle's own unhappiness out on me and Sophia. Is that a nice sentiment?

GRANDFATHER No; and I don't deny it may be true. But you could keep it to yourself, as Sophia would have done. And anyway, you too fell for it, didn't you?

JOHN (*laughing*) Pax!

GRANDFATHER But not yet . . . So it is not disinterested love that you have been wanting, but love from the pure in heart? There aren't many of us like that. And did you love Sophia like that?

JOHN No, damn me, thank you. But she did me I think. Well, almost.

GRANDFATHER So what now would she want for you. Think what her letter said. 'Your Sophia'. You have no more right to damn yourself than to damn your Uncle Rory. Even your father has had frustrations to contend with. And (*a grim smile*) of some of those I am not entirely guiltless.

JOHN On the whole I don't think he has done too badly. Rory does Papa's work and he got Rory's girl. I think I could live with Pa's frustrations, Grandpa. And he can have the estate back too now, if he wants.

GRANDFATHER (*can conceal his hurt no longer*) John!

JOHN (*subsiding*) OK. Sorry. I didn't mean that.

GRANDFATHER (*lightly*) I should hope not! (*Pause*) You're not to blame yourself for what has happened. And that's an order. (*Another pause*) She sent it back? (*looking at the Black Peacock still in John's hand*)

JOHN Yes. How did you know she had it?

GRANDFATHER You asked me if she could.

JOHN Sorry. Yes, I forgot. Yes, she sent it all back.

GRANDFATHER Because she had no more use for it. So you know how I'd feel if you gave me that back? (*Points to the Velasquez Water Seller*)

JOHN Love is handing on life, she knew too. But at a price.

GRANDFATHER Now we come to it: the Black Peacock, the water in the glass.

JOHN To her the water seemed alive, and the light through the glass, almost to speak. But Mozart made her think of beechwoods – of perfection with no understorey; Beethoven of oaks – our Saxon Oak – and oceans; Sibelius of endless lakes and spruce forests. Oh yes, and ice caps. While to me it's all just – no, not just – music. She went quite mad about a new mushroom to eat. Those white plates on spindles – Parasols – she said were sunshades on a Midi beach. Chantarelles were angels' trumpets. The cep boletus *was* a beefsteak. And she read somewhere that those red down-turned bowls with white blotches on them . . .

GRANDFATHER Fly agaric – weird and wonderful – and quite lovely.

JOHN . . . made you drunk and then blind. She looked quite queer when she spoke about them. And lawyer's wigs, those white johnnies with frills around them – they were a busy and pompous court. And stinkhorns – well, never mind . . . Things for her coalesced into thoughts bigger than the sum of their parts.

GRANDFATHER Everything interesting connected to something else that grabbed her into a bigger whole?

JOHN (*nodding*) For me they generally don't. Yet to me that picture – and the Peacock too in fact – wasn't just itself. It was the continuity of St Columbas at Bendor, and from you to me, with Father somewhere with that shadowy figure in the background. And it was Bendor coalesced with Sophia.

GRANDFATHER Not very complimentary of your father, do you think?

JOHN But you see, and as you almost said, I dropped the glass!

GRANDFATHER I wonder if it matters too much where the water goes, once we have or haven't drunk it? Whether it goes into a sewer or a spring, it'll end in raindrops? Or another Sophia?

JOHN There won't be another Sophia. Continuity is not repetition, nor can the future compensate for the past. There comes never again the same chance. Nor even the same end, though the series of events is never-ending. And people have an end too. Hence the need for Resurrection!

GRANDFATHER (*smiling*) You abstract too much and associate too little. Be a little more like Sophia. She would like that. Cannot she play the woods or her hair a cornfield? Try relating events to events, not seeing them as points in an endless recession. That way your past breeds your future. And Sophia will be borrowing your eyes.

JOHN Thank you, Grandpa; but for me music will always be music and Sophia Sophia. She used to say that you are very wise; and I can see that wisdom comes with accumulation. But I don't think I want wisdom. I need understanding not muddied by resignation. I want to know *why*.

GRANDFATHER All those 'I's'. You'll be very lonely.

JOHN Yes, very. Unless never. (*He goes out and enters the Den*)

(*John in the Den. Enter Madge*)

MADGE I know they've all been in. Job's comforters, the lot of us.

JOHN Nonsense. You have never given a word of advice in your life!

MADGE I am no meddler.

JOHN And no one meddles with you?

MADGE (*laughing*) They wouldn't get very far. Though some of them mean well.

JOHN Yes some, maybe. But I wonder of anyone knows what they think about serious things. How can you foresee the effects of what you say if you don't know your motives in saying it?

MADGE That's only the half of it. 'Motives' are only words after all; and how do you attach them to your feelings, to your guts? When I feel sick in the mornings, I think of my Henry on the Somme. Or maybe after all these years I just feel sick? So I don't take words for my feelings too seriously. Pain and passion drive them.

JOHN Now you are talking about feelings, not motives.

MADGE I was talking about how I come to terms with my feelings. I have yet to meet a motive in broad daylight, mine or anyone else's. But at night sometimes I think my only motive is self-preservation – which in the long run is anyway beyond me.

JOHN (*laughing*) You should have been a philosopher.

MADGE I don't talk much.

JOHN But you do laugh a lot.

MADGE Self-preservation. If you can keep on laughing, you never know where you can get.

JOHN And laughing keeps you going. You sly old thing, you've been giving me advice all the time.

MADGE (*laughing*) And remember, it's Easter tomorrow. (*exeunt together*)

End Act 2, Scene 2

ACT 2, SCENE 3

(*The Den. John is lying on an old couch.*)

JOHN (*dreaming in a condensed pool of light*) Tomorrow is Easter. It feels like just yesterday that it was Christmas. The promise. And in fact, it was Sophia yesterday. Yesterday was Christmas; tomorrow is Easter. A whole life. Winter to spring. There are seasons for God and Beast, but not for Adaptable Man, like an actor without a personality of his own. Easter tomorrow. Thus, the year is irreversible, inexorable. My for ever revolves around this – this recurring endless pointless dream, from which – the point? – there is no escape. Between yesterday and tomorrow. They all came, so that I can give some meaning to today. But they know they have nothing to offer: heaven is Sophia revived. So why kill her?

(*Enter Mother Ann*)

MOTHER ANN Who killed her? From asking that there is no escape.

JOHN Yes. I, even I only. But neither pain endured nor guilt admitted and forgiven purifies. It's true that fighting them can empower one part of you, but only at the expense of another part. Thus, the understanding of Providence is at best a half-truth.

MOTHER ANN Nobody accepts forgiveness except in the hope of love; and no one accepts forgiveness of sins, save in Faith of Resurrection.

75

JOHN So happiness is the fulfillment of the whole – seeing God everywhere but not needing Him? If I had met God in the Garden, what could I have said but 'You know Sophia, I think?' 'But you do not know Wisdom.' And He would have passed by on the other side.

MOTHER ANN Which Garden? Thinking it was the Gardener?

JOHN A coldness takes hold of me . . . a hermit crab without a shell.

MOTHER ANN Then at least you have a feeling.

JOHN The spring outside is my underwater world. If I belong, it's enemy territory. If I don't, it's a peep-show for empty speculation. In here Bendor and its knights and ladies are dried rose-petals to the mob, to me a battlefield with poppies as miserable as the trenches. Just as for them, outsiders, their high street is men trampling on each other's property and denouncing authority in the name of liberty and making up aimlessness to look like individuality. But not even Bendor is safe from the wolf pack. We starve ourselves to death. They will break in, only to find dry bones and faded portraits. And in turn they will turn against each other.

MOTHER ANN Unless you find – teach – the truth. (*exit*)

JOHN
   The fault of lords and ladies is not more terrible than the mortality of the mob.
   I, every I, have the one sea wandering in my veins – the wan sea wondering . . .
   The Minotaur stalks in his Labyrinth – curious, hungry and very proud.
   Fossils in light flown – nebula, fly and bat: rhythm of Okeanos has discovered you,

Like a crab overturned by a seagull's beak.
Still amber pinions, Icarus, oh my crusader, frozen in sunstone, steady your ribs crossed.
For many lives have lit your dead course here.
But your pall frames now a new, an unknown face.

(*Enter Madge*)

MADGE Or is Bendor only humans after all? And Sophia no more to be pitied than a girl run over by a salesman?

JOHN When Grandpa dies, will it be more than affection that stabs, and more than affectation to stand to attention. Is anything nobler than anything else – a hawk than a vulture, say, or that stag than a wolf?

MADGE If survival is proved to be the only excellence, then the thief uses solitude better than the saint, and excellence is a freak of dust in an almost dustless space. All is One. That's how we all feel. (*exit*)

JOHN Sophia, blessed be you – you can't survive. Bendor, you can't survive. God bless us all or not.

(*Suddenly John jumps up in a blaze of lights: now it's obvious he has been dreaming all along*)

JOHN So I come to the question. I have feelings: so what? What can be attached to them? Being unhappy I feel the need for what I call God. Or do I just feel? I will be answered! You have knocked the gilt off Bendor's frame. You have shown me every kind of loveliness and destroyed it; You have bundled me up in circumstances like a herd of bullocks through a narrow gate. And you do this across the world every day. But You have focused my curiosity. I glare at you now like a search light. There is no glass darkly between us now. I stare You in a duel face to Face . . .

77

Here is my gun loaded; and I have nothing to lose. Only You can restore me; and only You lose if You don't. Your blessed omnipotence makes You vulnerable. If I pull the trigger and my gun goes off You lose. If I die today, You are a ghost; and a ghost that goes through walls not as a dispensation of Your power but because You too cannot see them. I shall have proved that You don't exist; and thereby I shall have rescued my Vision of You.

Better a dead God than a callous God. So now the truth and nothing but the truth.

The price He knew, as the Samaritan sleeping rough, robbed penniless by beggars:

He gave His all abused right up to suicidal, in a last scream to be heard,

Like Kirillov to be free, mathematically Marxist, He proved, altruism saves progeny, though I die science' death childless –

In blind Faith's future over necessity victorious.

Amoeba becomes what it consumes: what if it can consume itself alone?

I am amoeba; fish ate me. I am fish; man ate fish. I am man; Man ate me. I AM; what am I?

The truth now! I shall light a match to surprise You.

(John removes the safety catch, lays the gun across a chair pointing at himself, pours a little glass of chartreuse in a toast to it. Then he picks up the gun, slips the Black Peacock in his pocket and marches out.)

End of Act 2, Scene 4

(*In the Library: Grandfather, Richard, Jeremy, Robin and Miranda. Grandfather gets Jeremy to hang the Black Peacock next to Raymond's Chinese prints*)

GRANDFATHER Thank you; and there she stays.

JEREMY Quite right. We shall see to it.

ROBIN Rather an eerie idea: Sophia the black widow?

MIRANDA (*quietly*) Either John bit himself or we ate him.

JEREMY I'd rather think it was us than him.

RICHARD Yes – murder is more healthy than suicide.

JEREMY John wasn't ill – but desperate, naturally. I think he was most worried about justice. (*All look round surprised*) I mean, well . . . (*confused*) . . . Sophia . . . It must have been someone's fault. He wanted to understand. Me too. Don't you?

GRANDFATHER And he took that darkness on himself.

(*An embarrassed pause*)

ROBIN I guess someone should go to John with the police and medics. Come with me, Jeremy?

JEREMY He didn't do it. I just know he didn't!

(*He rushes out, followed apologetically by Robin*)

RICHARD (*tense*) Touching faith! And I don't believe in justice either . . . Allah makes and Allah takes. You take or are taken – and you don't look back. That's why you can wish for your sons nothing but strength. But to punish yourself for what afterwards you feel you should not have taken . . ? That feeling of need – to punish yourself – is nonsense, horrible: the result of parental bullying in fact.

GRANDFATHER Thank you!

RICHARD That John was weak was bad enough. But that he was a martyr?

MADGE So you think John was weak? Suppose he left Sophia alone, not because he didn't want to go to her, not because he was afraid of you, Richard, or any of us, but because he thought, contrary to his inclinations and instinct, he should respect and obey his father?

RICHARD There is no virtue in that. We Normans grew great rebelling against our fathers.

MADGE You wanted John to rebel against you?

(*Re-enter Robin*)

ROBIN No more to do for John. They've taken John to the morgue.

MADGE (*repeating*) Richard, you wanted John to rebel?

RICHARD And it back-fired, I admit. Sadly.

MADGE Nonsense! I'm not letting you get away with that, Richard. You were jealous and paying John back! Or perhaps we are both right. John needed to find his own way. And you, dear brother, besides being jealous, wanted John to find it . . .

RICHARD (*suddenly openly angry*) I know what you're all doing – blaming me. OK. Alone I did it. The strongest head should bear the crown. Long live Robin St Columba.

(*For once Robin looks embarrassed and slinks out again*)

MADGE Smoke screen again!

GRANDFATHER Bendor rejects you both, father and son. The more vehemently you reject guilt, refusing forgiveness, the more deeply guilt becomes embedded and the uglier it deforms. God give John rest! (*exit*)

RICHARD (*turning his back on Grandfather*) Houses are women's talk. Women are necessary for procreation. Men decide the succession. Bendor is dead unless my family lives – in these few acres, last redoubt of Old England!

MADGE You must be rattled. You're not usually pompous!

(*enter Rory*)

RORY Right! I have dealt with police and all . . . Meanwhile you, Richard, may be a barbarian Crusader. But to make this old place crumbling into the present the scene of a costume drama, to amuse yourself . . .

RICHARD (*ignoring Rory*) In old days coral reefs were made of our bones. Now they are made of mock Tudor suburbs. Do you want to go semi-detached? And even if I am a barbarian – not a Norman except by blood – Bendor is a dead shell I can still use.

RORY I wish I could think you mad. (*exit*)

RICHARD You can say what you like about me and Robin; but he would never have done this!

MADGE Done what? Damn you – and damn your little red Robin too!

RICHARD More cute than John, like it or not!

MADGE Must we still take sides – bickering like Homer's Gods?

GRANDFATHER (*re-entering*) Olympus was too much for anyone's sanity. I too must go and rest. (*exit*)

RICHARD What does he know about Homer except nodding off? The only reading you enjoy, Madge, is about daughters of nineteenth century clergymen riding mules through China – intrepid Victorian busybodies rather like yourself.

MADGE Father was a scholar of sorts; and like me or not, I do mind my own business here. Why couldn't you leave John and Sophia alone? I think you only side with Robin to glorify yourself. God help the family if he does turn out like you!

RICHARD Would you rather have had John turn out like Rory? He would have for sure, you know. There is no pattern that makes sense; but there are any number of patterns that repeat themselves – and particularly in an old family.

MADGE Now, Richard, you have put your finger on what has been puzzling me: Rory is still alive.

RICHARD You mean, why didn't Rory kill himself years ago? Good question! It has never occurred to me to do so. For once, dear elder sister, you are a step ahead of me. Perhaps it was, I, as a younger brother, didn't have much of ally in an over-protective father, who expected too much of me! But if so, why not Rory?

MADGE Then please don't expect too much of Robin . . ! In fact I don't think anything would drive Rory to suicide. *Or* Robin.

RORY (*re-entering*) I heard that. It wouldn't and it hasn't. Has my dear brother been wishing us one by one into voluntary oblivion?

MADGE Everyone except himself.

RORY Not me – and I don't believe it of John, either!

RICHARD Sentimental ass! You just don''t want to accept the obvious!

RORY You were suggesting before I came back in – were you not? – that John was like me . . . In London, as the tube comes in, I often think to jump – a sort of vertigo. But I never do.

RICHARD It happens all the same.

RORY Not then at all the same. For me there would have to be something that gave me no alternative but to jump. But you are right: I am pleased you think me like John.

RICHARD For you, guilt!

RORY No! Because my impulse to jump, almost before I am aware of it, is overmastered by an immediate impulse not to. It almost feels as if the desire to jump is no more than the imagining of the moment of death, an acute sense of the possibilities of living and dying at the same time: no more than a functioning of curiosity. I don't think in fact anything or anyone could kill my curiosity – least of all myself.

MADGE Precisely.

RICHARD Are you quite sure that hell might not oversatisfy your curiosity, though you tell us you have lost your Faith – whatever that was? Or by losing it, are you absolved of hell too? A very nasty prospect, even I can imagine! But John's suicide wasn't vertigo, but a sense of guilt that I guess you must share. I call it suicide from natural causes. John finds himself guilty of a conspiracy to kill and executes himself, encouraged by a distaste of battling on.

MADGE Lucky for you then you don't believe in guilt! Too dangerous? I thought you were supposed to be the executioner. 'Alone I did it!' Guilty or not guilty?

RICHARD (*laughs at last uneasily*) Accessory before the fact perhaps. But anyway I don't believe in capital punishment either.

MADGE Thoroughly modern Richard after all!

(*Miranda has been standing unnoticed with Jeremy in the doorway for some while during this exchange; and now sits down very tired*)

JEREMY Pa, why did you do it?

MIRANDA Why did we send Sophia away?

RICHARD Rory thought he understood John; and they were too young to know their minds.

MIRANDA You weren't caring about them, either of you. You, dear Richard, were smarting over John's inheritance leap-frogging yours. And you, Rory, were busy 'regaining your Faith'. You know the poem you read me for your purpose? How did it go? 'Theodicy hangs the pendulum of dancing time . . ?' That's, was it, 'Theodicy, The Odyssey.' What on earth is a theodicy anyway?

RICHARD Justifying God to man. Impossible job (like justifying man to God!) and bloody cheek anyway! And you, dear brother, were climbing up the Cross to add your feather weight to His on the nails!

JEREMY I only know I shall miss them for ever. And we all should miss them. And they were happy.

RORY I wanted to get it right. And theories matter.

RICHARD Idle curiosity again.

MIRANDA We haven't enough to do!

RICHARD Nothing we can do now.

JEREMY You grown-ups – arguing in school corridors, and too old to learn!

RORY (*very quietly*) Very well. I wouldn't do it; and he didn't do it.

MIRANDA All right then, Rory: so your theory matters. So now you run along and prove it!

RORY Very well. I shall!

RICHARD Good for you, Em!

(*Rory and Madge look at each other very surprised and walk out, followed by Jeremy*)

MIRANDA I have no idea when you last called me that. So very long before these nine long months.

RICHARD I am quite fond of you, you know. Still. Come. (*He kisses her, roughly but expertly*)

85

MIRANDA I suppose I should have said, 'Not now!'

Richard You never have yet!

MIRANDA I always wanted you. But you confuse me. More now than ever. (*With a grin*) What are you up to?

RICHARD Nothing for once. I just didn't want you to think I wasn't very sorry.

MIRANDA Sorry? For John or yourself?

RICHARD You first and then me. But that's a start, you know.

MIRANDA Not much of one. What of John?

RICHARD Don't reject me. Not now. I must hold on to some one. I haven't been uncertain before.

MIRANDA And I trust, never of me, though you pretended. (*Hand on belly*) That always was part of your reluctant charm. For you never believed it. And Rory would never have wanted it otherwise.

RICHARD He was alone, not even God. So he invented you. Of course I never believed it. If I had there'd be no more good moods, believe me!

MIRANDA Why?

RICHARD I wouldn't want you to make love to anyone else.

MIRANDA Why? Go on, say it.

RICHARD I rather like you.

MIRANDA (*laughing*) So what do you want of me?

RICHARD You! I used to like the idea of myself cold and alone. Like an ice chip of a star on a frosty night. Or like the wind on the dunes. Even when I made love to you, I am thrusting you further from me, until you were pinned, a catherine wheel of a distant galaxy.

MIRANDA So I never touched you, even then?

RICHARD I was untouchable. (*Laughs*) Indestructible and contemptible – a devil turning slowly in orbit round myself. It might be nice to be a devil.

MIRANDA But you are not.

RICHARD After all this, John has shown me that I am not self-sufficient. If you rejected me now, as probably I deserve, God damn it, I shouldn't just be alone but damned lonely. So don't!

MIRANDA (*ironically but not unkindly*) Nice to feel one is wanted, after all. (*Pause*) So you think you may be human?

RICHARD But I still have no idea who? Nothing I say quite means what I want, even at the moment I say it. To act a part is to simplify yourself. So for example, John is a bit of an airy fairy softie – and content to have everything handed him wrapped in Christmas paper. So I act hostile as a foil. But I know I am jealous; and that helps my act more than somewhat. But all the time I know I love John a deal more than Robin, my creature. And perhaps that is all of it.

MIRANDA You wanted John; so you wanted him perfect!

87

RICHARD (*laughing*) A consistent egoist to the last! Almost. Even egoists can be robbed, even by themselves. And unlike devils, they die.

MIRANDA My Q. is, do you care more for the effects of all this on John or on us?

RICHARD John's last effects are dealt with. Sorry, I don't mean to be callous. But there is no virtue in grief, least of all as self punishment. Though I admit grief should focus the future. But I am in pain, like you – and I wish it would go. So far it blinds; and I am no wiser.

MIRANDA When were you ever?

RICHARD Just with you, no one else, I want to see the truth. I am looking death in the face, as John did. What did he see? Annihilation I cannot comprehend, though I can laugh at it. Laugh and be the devil. But self-annihilation? I feel with that thought very cold. There is no defence: I cannot laugh at it.

MIRANDA Was John's then a mute protest?

RICHARD Not directed at me. John wouldn't expect, or want me much, to notice. Nor is mine directed at Fate – another beautiful statue of smiling marble unlike anything that ever lived. Nor is mine at God? Did It look after Sophia or shut my brutish mouth?

MIRANDA Perhaps yes to both. You at least are speaking with a voice I scarcely recognise. Though once in the conservatory at that silly hunt ball – you know the one where they had taken it into their heads to have a chandelier with real candles?

RICHARD Which fell and set alight that frisky girl's dress. Oh yes, I enjoyed stamping on it stamping on it, right off her till her flames were quite out. Oh and then . . . Quite a striptease!

MIRANDA That night after, you talked as if love meant something.

RICHARD I was making polite conversation. After all we were engaged and in bed.

MIRANDA (*with a mock sigh of relief*) Richard is himself again. For a moment I was quite worried for you.

RICHARD So you think John was taking a pot-shot at God? Rather a fine idea – much better than mine playing the Devil. Maybe I underestimated John.

MIRANDA Well, don't you try it!

RICHARD Not my idea; so it would lose its point, wouldn't it? What gave you the bizarre idea anyway?

MIRANDA I couldn't bear thinking our John should destroy, betray – no, I don't mean betray: miss out on – well, life and everything.

RICHARD (*to her surprise kissing her gently this time, face and belly*) Love does mean something – or I am an outcast from myself.

MIRANDA (*doubtfully*) There's still Robin to cope with – and there'll be other shadows . . .

RICHARD Love me, Em!

End Act 3, Scene 1

(*The Den. Jeremy is staring out of the bay window. Robin enters quietly, not seeing him*)

ROBIN Oh! I didn't see you skulking there. I thought you'd be up with the cows.

JEREMY Oh! It's you. (*He turns his back to the window*)

ROBIN A fine view.

JEREMY (*not turning round, putting his hands over his face*) Wrong eyes. I wish no one could see it now.

ROBIN I do believe you're blubbing.

JEREMY I'm not the prep school sneak. Blubbing?

ROBIN (*coming closer*) Thought so – blubbing!

JEREMY OK. I'm going.

ROBIN That's as well, because I need to look for something actually.

JEREMY (*not listening*) What was that? I'm going to New Zealand.

ROBIN Running away!

JEREMY Not from you.

ROBIN Gracious of you not to stand in my way!

JEREMY Out there – look – our old red earth – blood money.

ROBIN I say – really. Just because . . . We're not all monsters.

JEREMY Did you do it? (*He has become truly formidable for a moment*)

ROBIN Do what?

JEREMY Kill John. You were there.

ROBIN You're crazy. And I was *not* there!

JEREMY You were. I spotted you nearby anyway, canoodling as usual with May. But though you'd have liked to, you wouldn't have the guts . . . It was contrary to nature: he couldn't do it. So come on – tell me what happened.

ROBIN No use running away. But anyway this place is not for you, though this place is part of you.

JEREMY Tell me!

ROBIN Face facts. What does it look like? (*looking round*) I know John's will is somewhere in here. (*He dives into the cabinet*) Ah, got it!

JEREMY Go away then, and take it, if you must. (*Robin stays, hovering*) Go away! (*exit Robin as Rory enters*)

RORY You shouldn't be here.

JEREMY John was my friend. Paying my last respects.

RORY I meant, I think you shouldn't wallow in our mud.

(*Jeremy nods as Rory exits*)

JEREMY (*alone, comes to front of stage*) Oyez – oh yes! I'm going to New Zealand. Good farming there and the soil there is not blood red – I hope.

GRANDFATHER (*has heard – enters the Den*) You'll be back!

JEREMY Oh, that. (*smiling*) Bendor's in my bones. But I want to break the chain.

GRANDFATHER Or the chains? Burying the past – or freedom?

JEREMY Or both together? Ghosts – we are full of them. In the house, in us.

GRANDFATHER As I said, you'll be back!

JEREMY (*a moment, a boy again*) Grandpa, he didn't do it. Say he didn't do it! (*He exits clumsily*)

(*Grandfather smiles and looks around, but stays on John's chaise longue. Lights down*)

(*Lights up. Still the Den. Rory has been sorting papers, now lies on John's chaise longue in precisely Grandfather's pose. But where Grandfather wears a green smoking jacket, Rory wears his rough and tatty tweed jacket with leather elbow patches. Enter Madge*)

MADGE It's a kindly room. I liked John's friendly chaos. You've been tidying papers? Tidy yourself up too, I suggest. Do make a job of it as John's advocate. That'll do you good too. But were they just brave words?

RORY Not about myself. About John maybe. We shall see. But I was taught, when there are two equal possibilities, believe the better and call it Faith.

MADGE Better than let the Church tell you which! Be Protestant first, to be Catholic afterwards? So back to basics now. Then earlier, you boobed badly!

RORY I boobed, as you so kindly put it, with the best of borrowed intentions.

MADGE So with damn-all Faith.

RORY Perhaps.

MADGE Never perhaps say 'perhaps' again! You lived with the You-and-Miranda-perhaps these fifteen years. Eyewash, when all you wanted was a mirror! So John is your mirror now.

RORY (*defensively*) Well, I'm doing my best now anyway.

MADGE I'll leave you to you and John. Have you seen Jeremy? There's no one to do a damn thing over Easter.

RORY He's doing the milking.

MADGE (*a bit deflated*) I wish he had told me.

RORY With the men off, he'd have thought you'd know. (*grinning*) We have trained him well.

MADGE He usually says.

RORY He's growing up. All this is enough to make anyone grow up.

MADGE Even you. (*She exits as Robin enters*)

RORY Is that you skulking? So you were coming to look around too.

ROBIN I couldn't make up my mind. It's a bit spooky really, dead man's shoes. Like that old ship found deserted on the high seas. What was it called?

RORY The Mary Celeste. Yes, it is a very positive nothing in this room. You find it mysterious?

ROBIN Curious, maybe.

RORY But not mysterious? Don't you want to know whether John killed himself, and if so, why?

ROBIN The why is elementary. If I'd liked Sophia like that and let her down . . . (*pause*) I *did* like her as a matter of fact.

RORY I thought May was more your thing. Or did you let them both down?

ROBIN I don't know. I don't know anything about anything.

RORY Liar!

ROBIN What has May got to do with it? And Sophia didn't rely on me for anything. Worse luck. I admit I didn't make things any easier for her. But that's different.

RORY How different?

ROBIN Responsibility versus opportunity.

RORY No! You betrayed her.

ROBIN She never trusted me, relied on me. She never even looked at me. Who was I to betray her? What was there to betray? Silly word anyway.

Rory Like 'guilt' to your father. Right! No more betrayals: you let down not Sophia but yourself.

Robin I didn't and don't think much about myself, only of what I want. I am only what I want; and if I don't get it, I don't see that I am anything at all.

Rory And you have got what you want?

Robin Yes, with a little patience, I have Bendor, I am Bendor.

Rory But you still have a brother.

Robin Grandfather wouldn't live long enough to do it. Besides, it isn't even his any more, but John's or taxman's. John made a will leaving everything of his to me. That of course includes the Estate and ultimately the house.

Rory So the will is what you were looking for.

Robin Actually, yes. It was in the bottom right there. He made it on his eighteenth birthday. He got Higgs and Mrs Higgs to sign it. I've seen it. And I've got it.

Rory But suicide invalidates a will.

Robin Eh? Surely not.

Rory Unsound mind. Balance of mind disturbed.

Robin Hell! I don't believe it. You're bluffing.

Rory By the way what has happened to your little girlfriend?

Robin What girlfriend?

RORY May Higgs. A generous-hearted and not a silly girl. What have you been up to? You were seen with her around the time and quite near – but not just 'heard' like Sophia with John. She hasn't spoken a word, your Auntie Madge says, since John died. Not to her mother, even. She goes round like an automaton, and an inefficient one at that. She keeps breaking dishes. Come on – out with it!

ROBIN I have no idea what you're on about. You must be just bluffing and fishing? Now that wouldn't very nice or Christian, would it?

RORY You may not believe it – yet – but you're about to get a couple of beautiful black eyes.

ROBIN Silly bluff again!

RORY (*hits him surprisingly efficiently*) That's one! Now suppose we get down to business. That mystery I keep talking about. And careful – you have only one black eye so far.

ROBIN (*defiant*) Ow! You had better be careful. If I can sneak about John and Sophia, I can sneak about dear Mama and guess who. I have letters . . . I expect I shall now.

RORY I regret even one black eye. You're not worth even a sore fist. Not even a poker player. You don't know to weigh the chances. Thick-skinned too. Do you really think that all a man and a woman can have in common is bed? Probably you do.

ROBIN Do you know, you bluff rather well?

RORY Well you, dear nephew, don't. Clinging to your father, we both know you are nothing. As empty as this room is, for all John's clutter. Born brain-dead. Why do you think he uses you? Because like a clone you can't answer back. Like the mirror, mirror on his wall, you are just a younger version of himself. He's terrified of getting old – and after that 'what dreams may come'. And no – you won't get Sophia or Bendor or anything else you want. I'm sorry for you. I would like you to get something. Perhaps we could do a deal?

ROBIN What deal?

RORY That mystery. No suicide note; so you'd expect it to be rigged to look like an accident. But, no. Cartridge bag, shells and shooting stick neatly on the other side of the fence, as if John was just about to get over it – so careless of him not to unload! But John's found twenty yards away with his gun still pointing in his face. It's incredible anyone could have fallen so neatly. Some one moved him and re-arranged him. John was posed. Robin, did you kill your brother?

ROBIN Oh, Uncle, really!

RORY I know for fact you weren't just near, but there. I didn't quite speak the truth. May admits she and you were both there together.

ROBIN You must be lying again. May wouldn't have said I killed John. Because I didn't!

RORY See what I mean? Silly little nobody falls straight into the first tuppeny-ha'penny trap ever invented by a detective writer. You have just admitted that you were there and you saw John die. You have only said you didn't kill him – which I anyway believed. So what of that deal? You want Bendor. I want the truth.

ROBIN Your thing about suicide invalidating a will. That wasn't true?

RORY Certainly not!

ROBIN (*grins admiringly*) That was clever.

RORY (*sharply*) No crawling, thank you! It doesn't work with me like your father. The truth if you please.

ROBIN One condition? You don't tell Father how you knew.

RORY Granted. Asking for that condition amounts to unconditional surrender.

ROBIN (*laughing*) Asking it was the family cowardice.

RORY Admitting your cowardice, knowing I'd not have told him anyway: family politics.

ROBIN Admitting my stupidity. Because of my cowardice I wasn't sure: I was knocked sideways.

RORY Anyway shut up admitting things. Get on with it!

ROBIN (*getting progressively tense as he relives the scene*) I wanted to see what I'd been missing.

RORY With Sophia?

ROBIN (*nodding*) I'd been thinking about that for a long time. So here was May naked on a bed dark green bed of periwinkles. Phew! She said she didn't want a rug – wanted to feel earth under her and me on top. To feel my animal. Suddenly she stopped and said, 'You do like me?' Rather nice that, since I am not. Then John's coming towards us muttering. His gun was broken over his arm, but loaded. He came right by us, not a yard from us and goes on a bit to put his bag over the fence by the stile, and turns back towards us. A jolt and he stops. Of all things recites one of his solemn poems, he thinks so marvellous, from last Christmas – rigid as a ham actor on stage, but out loud and distinct. (*He imitates his brother's pose and recites*)

'Be Protestant to be Catholic

Where suicide is sick-futile, there's maybe comedy not
    Of errors, but grown of ordure from tragedy –
    Time's inconceivable complexity,
Mycelium of life in death, hope's wars and Tommy's rot:

    Surprised by joy through troubles, best laugh through tears.
Come, eyeless in Gaza, so not before you have been through hell:
In head be and heart, and in passing, Emmanuel!
    Your Company in or out, Lord, no harmony here is,

Save both in Catholic from Protestant, and Prot
    In Catholic – with conscience in order, to be
    Whole selves, not fearing not to offend our peers . . .
Rings radiating single out the Christmas Bell.

All form is discovery of the One:
Speech from the dance of the hunt;
Prose from mementos of verse;
Comedy from memory of pain;
Catholic living from Protestant conscience.'

Next – John sort of relaxes, as if taking a bow after performing to an audience, then doing an encore:
    'Prot and Catholic can't live side by side,
    Not each seeing themselves groom and bride:
    For his conscience, his root –
    From which she sprouts her shoot:
    They split Christ with their matriage denied.'

A short pause – then:
    'Learn through tragedy
Faith head high spinning. Turn
    Faith's pain to comedy.'

Now he does bow deeply, somehow mockingly: 'So now in
response, Your miracle for John St Columba on the count of
three . . . One: A miracle or I shoot myself. Two: slither out from
under Your stone, God'. (He points his gun at himself.) 'THREE!'

    Spirit exhausts to
Entropy. None dares repent
    Sans Resurrection.

    One same path: tragic
To comic, Protestant to
    Catholic sense of life.

    Comedy divine is
Your Injustice justfied
    By Resurrection!'

John cocks his gun.

          'Aaron's Rod
Your social animal, Lord, I must speak with you.
    Forgive, pray, this intrusion my one last time.
    My shambled decline observing from my prime,
You know how even my progression refines Your view

    Of Your Creation by my enfeebled joys.
I am and of Your Company, Mind unworthy mine:
Caduceus, thyrsus and Aaron's rod we raise; we shine,
    Ride singing sands through desert traffic noise.

Were every grain Your angel, no deeper we'd pursue
   Your music, more joyful His Lacrimosa climb
   Sore wounded, ancients and infants, girls and boys,
Who mocking tragedy Your comedy divine.'

And then he sees us! 'The miracle! Roll up, roll up!,' he says. 'See
the miracle, the true lovers! Ho-ho!

   Failed the rule of the people? So what?
   Idiot, trust in the Big Man? Bigot!
   Round your neck, Death's a rope;
   To climb up with, It's hope.
   Christ begotten fascist risen is not!

   So Big Prot on Jacob's Ladder – klimax, climax!
   Ho-ho! Am I to piss on God just because half my family are
      pseuds? Theodicy, the Odyssey!'

And he fires over our heads, first one barrel, then t'other: 'That's
for justice and that's for truth!' He runs back to the fence for shells,
reloads, runs back towards us – and trips! As he falls, both barrels
go off in his face. Blood all over us. Christ! (*Then in a small voice*)
That's all, I think. (*Suddenly recovering himself, adds with a shy grin*)
Father, I have sinned.

(*Enter May*)

RORY Thankyou for responding to Inquisition. I asked May along,
in case you didn't come clean.

MAY Not very nice of you though, little chicken, to kiss and tell.
You're through!

ROBIN For now, yes, I suppose. But you liked me then, didn't you? So who knows? Maybe May?

(*Laughing, he catches May's eye, despite herself*)

End Act 3, Scene 2

ACT 3, SCENE 3

(*The Dining Room*)

MIRANDA When did you learn midwifery?

MOTHER ANN One day you'll cease to be surprised about what nuns know about women. But it was extremely careless of you to be left alone.

MIRANDA I think I might have managed. I am a mother too, Mother Ann.

MOTHER ANN Might I be godmother then? To another Sophia?

MIRANDA Yes. An odd coincidence, you being here for both our recent . . . events.

MOTHER ANN Coincidence? I heard when the funeral was to be. I too wanted a second chance, you know. And had it never come? We plod on. Nothing comes directly; but most things come the wrong way round, if we are given the time. Not even tragedies are tidy, nor final either – except for theatregoers. How I did love the theatre!

MIRANDA And you a nun? Why?

MOTHER ANN Worst possible reason. A man. So I had to lie my way in.

MIRANDA And you never confessed?

MOTHER ANN Of course I did, but not till it was too late to matter. Anyway I never doubted my calling.

MIRANDA I suspect you're not just for once being immodest. You aren't normally frank about yourself, that is.

MOTHER ANN I hope I wasn't trying to be interesting. I was giving an example of complexity. Not even my vocation was neat, though I never doubted it. I was softening you up. You want to talk about John.

MIRANDA Please.

MOTHER ANN It wasn't suicide?

MIRANDA No. A silly accident.

MOTHER ANN Then what are you fussed about?

(*Miranda stares open-mouthed at Mother Ann for a long moment*)

MOTHER ANN I didn't say, 'What are you grieved about?'

MIRANDA You do see things simply after all.

MOTHER ANN Only if your understanding is complex can you be both simple and right. Suicide requires a different kind of prayer. (*Cars are heard returning*) Your family is back. God bless you, my child – children!

(*She hurries out. The Family find Miranda alone on the couch with her baby*)

RICHARD Good Lord – Andromeda alone on rock with dragon.

MIRANDA She isn't a dragon. She is your daughter.

RICHARD Let me see: daughter or crumpled handkerchief? Sophia of course. (*An awkward pause*) Well, that's over. Save in the City, I have never been to a happy funeral before.

MADGE Then you owe Rory a vote of thanks.

RICHARD Probably I do. But why can't we leave anything unsaid in this damned family?

MADGE Generally because you haven't meant it!

RICHARD Pax!

MIRANDA Vobiscum.

RICHARD Good Lord – the crows haven't got you at last?

MIRANDA Mother Ann did give a little practical help. But I'm not dead yet. Nor is our Sophia.

JEREMY No one you are fond of and used to ever is.

MADGE Including John.

RICHARD (*surprising everyone*) Certainly including John!

ROBIN (*standing around ill-at-ease*) Can I have a drink?

RICHARD At five? Damn-well wait! Or offer your mother something at least.

MADGE (*laughing*) That's right: toughen him up!

RICHARD No need for everyone in this family to be as bloody rude as I am. Go on: ask her what she wants.

ROBIN Mother?

MIRANDA (*suddenly showing her tiredness*) A quiet exit, if you don't mind.

(*Rory quickly arranges. Robin looks on, helplessly attentive*)

MADGE Well, I'd better be off to make some tea.

(*Exeunt save Richard*)

RICHARD (*left alone in the Dining Room talks across the divide to Grandfather, in the Library*) Well, here we are. Some Norman blood spilt; but Normans should build things and rule people. John was never true to type. He would never have come to anything.

GRANDFATHER Look who's talking. And where now was there to go? On to the land? You'd make peasants of Bendor's St Columbas? But this rump estate would never support three families, you know. Suppose John had been a don at the family college. Would that have been so bad? Robin might have got his way with May here I presume? You haven't bred him up for much else. Jeremy, whom you took no notice of . . .

RICHARD Jeremy was obviously OK. New Zealand will suit him.

GRANDFATHER Like Samuel Butler: he may even turn out the best philosopher among us yet. Jeremy will be no trouble: he could make his way anywhere as a farmer already – here or anywhere else.

RICHARD You're watering us down. 'We belong hereabouts and hereabouts belongs to us.'

GRANDFATHER Not much left nowadays – thanks to Labour's '48 raj! Crop your grass too hard and it becomes a dunghill!

RICHARD Bad agri-theory! Dunghills are very fertile, though I accept some biological overtones. Bendor does smell somewhat. But at least Rory has shown it wasn't suicide. I admit that wasn't a bad family effort.

GRANDFATHER So you feel that lets you out? If it had been suicide, you would have blamed yourself – contrary to your very best Nietzchean principles. Admit it!

RICHARD (*grinning*) Between us girls.

GRANDFATHER We could say we have been lucky. It might have been a worse funeral. But now what?

RICHARD Bendor's tot-tot-tottering. The Estate was John's. How will Robin pay the taxman?

GRANDFATHER The Devil take him! 'Men not walls make a city.' Yes, that is a crib. But I know umpteen people the exciseman has turned out who have made better limpets than we have in this glorious old place. Suppose we are turned out, this old treasure will be opened to the public, to make what they can of it. They can't do worse than us! But the public in fact prefers to view us in our walls – still walled up, so long as we don't do anything. That annoys them, though I don't see them doing any better than us!

RICHARD They can't make anything alive of Bendor, any more than you can give an altarpiece a home in a museum. Bendor belongs not to St Columba, or some other tourists' saint in a holy bogus precinct, but to St Columbas!

GRANDFATHER You have thrown it away anyway. The sad Red Indians in their mean reservations just die out on hooch. We are dying out likewise from lack of will to live. Your pompous pose of 'toughening John up' – what have you achieved? You have meanwhile left Rory to run the Estate; and that's only half a job as he does it, anyhow!

RICHARD Father, you should have spoken like this two decades ago. Instead of showing you despised me. I had some feelings then, I think. I have signed off, hoping my sons might do something.

GRANDFATHER I do despise your self-pity. You were born with a brain, unlike, I sometimes fear, your precious Robin. You'll be telling me next you are all my fault for starving you of Daddy's love? 'Your parents fuck you up: they don't mean to but they do'?

RICHARD I couldn't have put it better than the poet! But I have never said it. (*Now angry*) I'd rather tell lies than be disbelieved telling the truth! You have always been so infuriatingly wise. Why couldn't you have done something yourself?

GRANDFATHER Not my turn – now, anyway. Having failed with you and Rory – though not, thank heaven, with Madge, I tried with your eldest son, John. And you sabotaged him.

RICHARD So you played the guru.

GRANDFATHER You can adopt a role without play-acting. And if you had wanted to talk, I was here. (*With an odd smile*) I am always here.

RICHARD Big Daddy will haunt us?

GRANDFATHER That I don't know. But Bendor will.

RICHARD (*laughing*) Robin will survive whatever happens and whatever he does. But I am sorry Bendor's going – for your sake.

GRANDFATHER Bendor will survive too, no thanks to you. You didn't notice that character with whiskers growing out of his nostrils? Never mind who he was: this is the point. (*He pulls out the Water Seller from behind a bookcase*) There please, where we can see it well-lit. (*They put it together, neither stepping out of his territory, over the fireplace*) Velasquez – didn't you know? Sophia loved it so much she was convinced it was real. So she combed our little archive room, for just an hour, for Raymond 1's file, when he brought the oil back from the Peninsular War. She was doing Spanish (with her Greek), you know for A-Level. Lo and behold – the docket said 'One of an identical pair of bodegones by the artist'. All I had to do was follow her up. The quality of the painting – and Bristle-Nostrils' reputation as an expert – did the rest. It'll have to go of course, like most of our land – though I hope to a British museum. (The National Museum of Scotland is sniffing.) But we'll get a modern copy, for remembrance of Sophia at least – passing on life, her life, at a price. Enough for the Devil and the excise man.

RICHARD A copy's not the same. Not Bendor. You live history, which is not a copy on a wall.

GRANDFATHER Nor is history stage drama. No Romeo and Juliet here, but John and Sophia. But Bendor is not forfeit.

(*Exit Richard, enter Madge into the Library. For the next sequence lights go down till only fading firelight visible*)

MADGE Fire worship again.

GRANDFATHER Not a bad religion: Pramanatha, Prometheus . . . Best, though, might be to domesticate oneself, like cat, dog, aurochs, horse and fire?

MADGE Self-worship again!

GRANDFATHER Were we good, we'd be as gods.

MADGE What's good? I mind my own business and run things and myself off my feet. If I run myself hard enough, I'll burst before I get old.

GRANDFATHER So for me, no solution?

MADGE Not now. Had you wanted to stay young, you would have run here. But you didn't?

GRANDFATHER Didn't I, though? But not what was no longer my turn.

MADGE So you get a family of heathens – undomesticated I suppose you call it?

GRANDFATHER You are being very hard on a poor old man.

MADGE (*with a warm smile*) You know I . . .

GRANDFATHER Don't mean it?

MADGE Of course I mean it – and thank you! (*She hurries out still smiling and bumping into Rory*)

GRANDFATHER So now what, Uncle? Always the uncle!

RORY We work, as Vanya would say. Good night. (*exit*)

End of Scene 3, Act 3

ACT 3, SCENE 4

(*The Den*)

GRANDFATHER (*alone on John's chaise longue*) So I had no excuse, acting the outsider? I wanted not to intervene, not to break freedom's pattern. 'Self-determination,' said I. 'Like God?' I asked. (*humming*) 'It ain't necessarily so.' Two possibilities: always God forgives, restores. But, One: God relies on probabilities – the bad outweighed by the good plus one, his casting vote. Or, Two: He might by fore-knowing (not ordaining) events – not just here but in eternity – construct a complexity we cannot conceive of, out of what looks to mortals the endless strands of coincidence, so that everyone has an equal chance of . . .

(*He has fallen asleep. Enter John*)

JOHN Of redemption achieved and accepted. Theodicy!

GRANDFATHER Only the unimaginable hugeness and complexity of such a universe of universes prevents anyone from considering this possibility. That and everyman's endless everyday traumas. But maybe God does not consider suffering – even of His Son! – as the worst of evils. But anyhow God as idle spectator is no third possibility! Sad Lucretius watching from shore the tumbling sea? Always better to tumble in it! My play! (*As a blind man sleepwalking, Grandfather collects his manuscript and flings it in the fire, then returns to the chaise longue*) I let no one know I wrote us up. So let that Old Man have the last word! With John: it cost him more!

JOHN
   You are my force diminished, diminishing me;
   So I shall not be for ever singing.
   Composed, I leave your song, a flutter of leaves;
   And where they fall, the sober wind exulting,

Till each melodic line resolves to silent logic
A life stilled in ether, time hammocked:
An arc suspended between the poles,
Time sleeps with my angel enfolded;
And in a serpent-ring they dream –
Like lovers occasionally – the same dream
Of waters undisturbed fresh and smooth stones,
Of opals darkening on the skin and dry white wine.
Children know this fragrance, which goes
Before they come to name it; and men
Remembering prefer beautiful things
Not to be explicable, and even tolerate suffering
Because it is not explicable, when frequently
Suffering could have been prevented.
This then is Faith: the lutinist beneath the beech at last
Achieves perpetuum immobile.

(*The grandfather clock hiccups in preparation for striking midnight*)

Hark, Faustus, the striking! So fine it down, man, to the count of
twelve . . .

Wild Time

Last night I dreamt a petty theft – mine without shame.
  I stole, for my garden new planted, hedge Eglantine,
    That lives round Nature's time, Its need not mine . . .
Conversion! I live with her now in freedom, none now may tame.

  For Bendor's was the oasis that none might share.
Our waters the deserts needed and others', for Eden's birth.
Nostalgia is anamnesis; and all One's garden, Earth.
  Else we're space junk, memento of Gaia's despair –

111

Collisions' divisions disperse to entropy; our game,
Charade? I trod of cultural greed no line,
No limit, so no respect: we've now no heir –
Save with us the All's for One, the one for all: no dearth!

GRANDFATHER

The Ides of March

(*'Vixi naturae satis vel gloriae'* – *Julius Caesar*)

Caesar was tired – and tired of Rome. He had his star
In Its eternity before him, but knew
He nature of Its glory? For the few,
Their person shines; for fewer the Person's whose they are.

The hunt is on. They'd kill him he knew, the East
With West who could have united; but greater the infection
Of Greater Rome? What slicker knives beyond correction
Betray their greater Emperor: what pettier Beast

Its Gaia's beauty? Oh, who was Caesar where Alexan
der failed? Spread limbo his panoramic view:
Man raped Persephone till all life ceased
With joy of Justice. What penitence sans Resurrection?

Freewill grows virtue
On Faith's resigned rejection
Of everything else.

Fear sad Earth leaving
Content, not folk here telling
What joys there I find!

Do happiest best: find
Resurrection hope. Patience:
Take others with you!

112

My Helen – to smile and be smiled on,
Glory from giving to receive again,
And You! Till I will Your will, Your hand on my gut.

For when I twist, You are twisted,
That I may be ready for the moment sans extension.

    Family Portrait staged
   As inscription encrypted
    Phaistos Disc immured.

TWELVE

(*Grandfather suddenly leaps up in a blaze of light and falls back dead.
John runs to pick him up, followed on stage by Sophia and the whole cast,
bowing*)

ALL *Resurrection!*

CURTAIN

Sartre's Inn (*for Gabriel*)

At our Aeschylus Homerid zoom,
You cried, 'World's End – Promethean Doom!'
  No one said a word,
   As if no one had heard –
A huis clos already no room?

1 Misfit

A misfit born clubfooted, so too big for the womb,
  With Jove in Leo for Justice' horoscope
  In Empire wounded, scarce was I vouchsafed hope
Of easy passage through this world to the next, via tomb

  Serene and decorous. . . Petrel of surf-crowned seas,
First find vocation, looking, listening; do avocation
Well; doing ever better studying animation:
  In peregrination alone your loves you please.

Vocation – first full-lipped kiss (and so taste of doom);
  Next avocation, the upward slippery slope
  Defining, for animation's widening ease
Of view up peregrination's dogged last elation . . .

2 Grandma's Footsteps (*for TSE & PP*)

In starting, Man's end: communication, community,
    Communion. Pilgrimage, Man's progress to
    Reversal. We have talked, together lived, to pursue
The Lord – good, better, best: It's wisdom to see

    In union beginning – human evolution,
Now scarce begun . . . Demeter's steps to integration,
The palinode: as hers seen, our investigation
    Frustrates free will, the joy of search. Solution?

To childhood's intimation of immortality
    Cling dogged and work! Courage – elation, too!
    Your pains and others' lies aren't your pollution.
No mystery: the mystic day-to-day is incarnation.

3 First Word

From night to night sky's progress for in common of the day
    The growth and use of heritage: the word
    For mining first of language, undeterred
By universal strangeness. Life programmed survives that way,

    As all the World were birdsong or a view,
And living already in It one half-heard conversation,
From birth at dawn to grasp the sole investigation,
    How all at once is many and one, both new

And old, as determined by probability to weigh
    In freedom: the call of wise Athena heard –
    To find and show what's thought best for the few
Rules best for one and all – democracy's oblation.

4 Reith in Upper House

Yet suasion keeps silence: don't tell 'em they don't know how
    to vote:
    That way they think (not their incompetence!)
    Lies tyranny. Not how they vote their sense
Of worth, but having It and taking part. Remote

    Their sensibility of everyday. They're free
From algorithms, entropy, polarisation,
And reefs of circumstances that jut out from frustration
    As consequence of responsibility.

They vote and basta! Their bastions, they seldom note,
    Stay oligarchic, beyond control of voters – defence,
    The media, Civil Service, Judiciary:
So Parliament needs a Second House – for truth's gestation.

5 The Vote

For each the All's to design in sign and sound: my art
    At midday refines desire – all's yours, yet mine:
    Creatures ere apogee their paths define,
Though called to account for their full orbit ere they depart.

    Youth stamps on eggs: old rule sans heart is worse.
To write a play to play but as author is self-immolation;
A score for others in play to grow themselves is creation.
    In youth self-doubt earns no respect. A curse –

Self-interested votes without self-knowledge tears polis apart.
    Drifts age secure content with slow decline . . .
    Let Commons mixed actions decide, so senate rehearse
Before and after expedient next age's preparation.

6 The Hoopoe of Aristophanes
(*for Uncle William and Grampy H W*)

Hamas and Likud unite in fear: so Two-State hate
   Their Palestine; Israel, Man's Holy Land.
   Greek Speaker Epops Upupa led Rome's band
As pedagogue; now Israel's, the bird needs lead debate

   For fare down daily, as then too in upper air
For wisdom. Yet Gaia's atmosphere is but one Station
For needs all settling, respecting in neighbourly migration
   In market and fare their Lady Mother fair . . .

Year Zero: Rome, Athens, Jewry had reached the solid state
   To claim creative change, as yet unplanned
   For Innocents by sicarii. Do, dare,
Your best, what, never enough, counts most in desperation.

7 Parliament International of the Air

The middle years – family, a hopeful sufficiency
   While all suspended ex cathedra see
   Walls closing in round Gaia, culture's gravity
Imploding. We sit back, brood on the FT.

   World ruin: climate, UN, the Bomb, AI,
Wars, misery, disorder . . . Sweet children but desolation
We leave: repent we may – for them no consolation!
   We are even too old to act or fight. We try

Our best. So PIA for Gaia and one humanity?
   Unique experiment: priority
   Inhuman; one for all we live or die
And all for one – re-animate man's incarnation.

8 King in Parliament

Where'er, there's but one Air for the birds in Parliament free –
    Shepherds and Commons, Angels and asses, King
    And Lords, in round the manger beckoning –
Assembly no more everyday or stranger than the Tree

    Where's room for natures all, more than we know,
Could man but trust repenting in rehabilitation.
In fear of knowing and being known, from penetration
    Mental we shy, with what AI can show

Robots, content . . . Via empathy to telepathy
    Both weak and lovely in Gyges' ring
    Let's see unseen, be seen unseen – earn, lo,
Here There anew grown up among children, reanimation!

9 Rothco

Walls closing in . . . that ghosts walk through – curtain or Veil,
    We stare through too. Impenetrable night
    No sentry sees, but shards of shattered light,
As Rothco paints It. In death's redoubt high-tech will fail

    To tell or tally: I know there to revere
No shiny widgets glib (brave new communication),
But Mind's untapped mycelium, that in relation
    Grows all things distant to one humus near.

What fearsome bogey to every mind each other's tale
    Opens? To know each other all fear would blight
    Their loves. No choice now but trust the pneumosphere,
Forgiveness understanding towards new incarnation.

10 Storm Petrel

Today tweets David Peter's water-walking bird.
    Kissinger dies. We buy our Advent Tree.
    On Mousa sick cats purr. Mortality:
In kitchen outside the forest giant's falling heard.

    Broch ringing round the moon foretells bad weather . . .
Our fault, at point of no return from desolation,
We leave behind. But pilgrimage, our consolation
    In Company; so moments stick together.

Lord, staunch the pain unbearable – on all else, joy's Word
    Heard call Its kindness down. Man's task, to free
    The common pain; grows life sphere of one feather:
Communion, community, *then* communication!

        Gaia's Golgotha,
        Launchpad to erehwon:
        No room in the inn.

11 May Day M'aidez!

May Day m'aidez! Why's not the spring pole dance still taught –
    Lives plaited perfect interleaved? We ran,
    You called: You had your girls; You were the Man.
Youth's innocence is not the starter's gun, but the medal sought . . .

    None blest till forgiveness; no actor before the play.
The drama the God's, Greek always knew that donned the mask.
We improvise. For His the scenario; ours the task.
    If His the final scene, we win the day,

Shown cursing how to love – till heresy now: we thought,
    Ours theatre and universe to scan,
    Lost with no prayer to focus for us our way.
'Speak to Me; why do you never speak?' It's You now ask.

12 The Star Imperative of Immanuel Kant

From Prussian to Russian, Koenigsberg to Kaliningrad:
    Their slipway to the common sea . . . So Kant
    Both international peace's hierophant
Makes best by general discipline enforced the sad,

    And universal pacificist, the holy
Self's conscience? What mind, though, keeps together good's
      increase,
If not the sacrifice absolute of lonely peace?
    Love only makes done duty kind, so wholly

Welcome. Diplomacy wars delays but to worse from bad;
    Star claimed sans Its whence and whither leading is cant:
    To choose good's means prescribes but pathway solely.
Spin there the kaleidoscope of duties that ever please!

      Homo, God's mistake,
    Out of love Who gave us choice,
      To love or love not?

      Point-nine-recurring:
    I must arise and go now.
      Christmas never comes.

    Conscience commands last
    Truth grows Itself not. In the east
      Lasts never Easter.

13 His Nursery Rhyme

Our Father, who put up with me long enough Thy nursery rhyme
    To learn – as I come out, teach me Your Mind!
    You gave me Thy toys to spoil: be not unkind.
In Voyager on golden disc I beat Bach's time:

    What more, to escape myself and eternal lies?
Raft sail, brave heart, to trade winds set for auld lang syne,
To enjoy our next extinction in prescribed decline
    Anthropocene? Or may I hope to rise?

Humiliation now wisdom made by Love sublime
    Forgiveness, shown land in freedom lined
    As weakness scorned, yet survival in wild surmise,
Departs Platform Cloud Zero on the platinum line.

        He's with us, Kingdom
        Within us: It was, didn't feel,
        Like that. That's the Faith!

        Am Sonnenabend (*for Peter & Sophie in W2*)

What goddess, Yolanda, coming through the leaves
    At sunset framed, you love,
    If not yourself above?
What you're up there not knowing is what grieves.

What person framed in theatre on this wall,
    Persephone, descending
    In new bones these your beauties ending,
Would you create your past sins to forestall?

121

14 Grammar of Truth (*for Paul Cook @OW*)

Grips sudden as earthquake Primordial Scream I learnt to ask
    Where God is not, since statesmen, as man is weak,
    Call any change reform, if they but speak –
As if no living prospect, no purpose in common task.

    All seek in confession of doubt His Company,
In media universal, TV news, pub quizz.
Denial's fear bars claim to sustenance invis-
    Ible, by want shown needed. 'Democracy'

Demeaning we chorus, cacophony of many to mask
    The folly of all but Him. Go inmost seek
    Your justice – sure, failures preclude no unity
Of search. The unthinkable is not: so Judge there is!

        Tight sails hence, Bay Star!
        Our gods with you, travellin' far,
        Where'er, Paul, you are?

15 Tiresias' Master Class

'Don't blame us, the blindfold: we did not know . . .' '. . . Save
    what must be!'
    '. . . Our future.' 'For living that's always enough.' 'The will
    We lacked.' 'Tiresias saw nothing, until
His courage. Now he's blind Homer!' 'Man owns no mystery,

    Save self-deception?' 'No faith, boy, save in self grounded!'
'Cruel choice, the creative ignorance we must admit!'
'Imagine, disciples, the pain in sculpting the Faith to fit
    His Face – when growing up you were sore wounded!'

'Thank God, though knowing I cannot feel The Cross!' 'But He
    Would have It no other way, the Snake to kill.'
    'Don't wait and see?' 'Prepare to be astounded:
Imagine the pain being made your last identikit!'

16 Orchard Waters

House spring, monks' carp stew to Bridge-on-Willie, my last stand:
    New arboretum, a moment's permanence.
    The busy river contains the resonance
Of myriad voices, that goldcrest and dipper echo, from land

    To sea, in memory's single conversation -
Creation's icon to Saxon, Norman, Sir William
And back . . . The Avenue felled I hardly walk now, and ham,
    As loving Lear, their usurped conversation.

I have heard It all, and shall again, to understand
    In anamnesis wonder's step to sense,
    And Faith's to humility in shame – elation,
I am particle inalienably of His I AM!

A Day at Wyld

    More's Wyld Mulberry
    After half a millennium
    Seeds a daughter tree.

    Rubbishing Rafah
    Rubble Netanyahu bins
    Land Law Holocaust.

    Greed's holocaust seeds
    Preserve! – for ground reseed(ced)ing
    Holocaust prepares.

17 Off Picol's Photograph

His Substance is to make to love; my Faith's a smile:
    Screwed up my Mappa Mundi in memory
    Last night a photo of background telepathy –
A two-year-old, young woman now, of simple guile,

    Das Ewig Weibliche: that selfsame greeting
Of all my Graces, but individual, that showed
Me worth as Ganymede and swept me up in code
    Enlightenment remorseless to their next meeting,

As Darwin with Annie on evolution's unmeasured mile
    Of broad savannah's brute migration . . . They free
    And beckon, those searing flashes of lightning fleeting,
And with St Elmo's Fire long after light our load.

18 Ahoy, Boys! (*for Ed and Edmund*)

Ahoy, buoys Wyndham lost – sons Ed, Esteban, John –
    That should have been heirs' anchorage! Where now?
    We flying dutch port nowhere, bow or prow:
First natures boxed, we dance to winds' choregicon.

    So what of them that haul us in their wake,
Unwilling-curious their voyage to rehearse,
That uncompleted is both blessing and our curse?
    Their loss forsaken, our mean selves we forsake

For double love: a stern elation where they're gone
    And giddy freedom – everywhere's nowhere! – allow
    Eternity by moments. For them we fake
Their journeys, to explore their endless, empty universe.

19 Orchard Open Day

Monks' watercourse – stews, moonpond, arboretum, stream;
   Two courts – Cistercian and Perpendicular;
   Four 'wow' rooms, solar, peacock, hall – but far
Most lived in for Harriett shall English Drawing Room beam,

   In wifely comfort, the Eighteenth Century,
Where we did plays and concerts – and with friendly laugh
Bid happy them farewell, back to their own home path.
   (But ours: hard work and a distant melancholy . . .)

Tombed Florence, fleatrap and striptease – what stories! –
   Wokky's soft scream,
   'For Edmund ill, let me through please!', the Wyndham star
Fallen from my window to build a harbour: we
Ghosts, wanted to show them round: they ask no autograph.

20 A Poet's Diary

Blue Diary ended, Open Day is open book.
   May's m'aidez done to no one's interest,
   I burst with gratitude for friends and rest
My case. I found the Truth and told It, where none shall look,

   I think, of Family, readers . . . That's not my task,
Not being a leader; and all must find their way. Correction
Of proofs is not of self or others. History's election
   Tombs others' choices. Past joys is all we ask.

I am one more stone to walk on. The pilgrim's trail I took.
   Sit, Stranger, on me a moment. Lay down your test.
   Sir William's Orchard planes fly over you, mask
Your duty. Your end – this dying world's – your Resurrection!

21 The White Goddess

(X II III D xxii =? obit 2nd March 1522 – for PP)

I staggered up Down Walk to Mother Shipton's Stone,
    From Harriett's woodwind Mozart in E-flat,
    (K.482, E's speakers, Eve's gram). I'd sat
Where Ma played Bach for Mozart Blackbird to intone

    His rising scale save seventh, past Pa's chair
(Beech stump next Pond 'neath ilex), past Roselyne buried there,
(Red hyacinth with blue), to Mother's Stone Circle bare
    And solo in wreath of forbears round her year,

The bearing Tree, her present moving poles alone –
    White Witch, she knows herself Its face (that's that!)
    And moon eclipsing sun. Behind the glare,
Before It, the uncreated Light is everywhere.

22 The Last Day (for Lucy)

I pity often God's disappointment; but today
    I knew Him young to smile His children's joy.
    I feared myself no fool: I am a boy,
To savour ridicule past envy as a play

    Of honour. I am no naive innocent;
But You are – the Idiot infectious as a dew
Outlasting time as memory and baby's poo,
    In moment's elixir Creation spent.

You saw It all: the possible, enough; the ray
    Of epilept enlightenment destroy;
    No martyrdom excess of love resent . . .
Just once today, My Lord, I was as old as You.

23 QI (*H&W on leaving OW 6th June '24*)

To be, each he or she, love It or not, must be
　　Their own religion, to choose their minstrelsy.
　　I play the tourist of lovelier gardens, free:
No rose bower's mine unless I tend It, she with me.

　　Lo, better our six foot square than all the tea
In China, with briar rose in hedgerow from bud hip see
Its bush to birth – Its history, my history:
　　It's freedom, acceptance of necessity.

So sing I, and like that gnomon count my hours. For we
　　By rapt attention compose eternity
　　Of moments, chaos distilling to harmony.
Where I am quaerens Intellectum, It must be He!

24 Leavings

What I have writ, I have written: there's dignity in death –
　　In weeding and washing up. With love we leave
　　No leavings (some trees, clean plates), not what we grieve.
No evolution here: 'Move on,' the prophet saith.

　　Desert and concrete we made of wold and weald;
Robot of mind; vulgarity of art; and pain
Of toil and deadened soil; of work, no peace in gain
　　Of joys: in Eden, nakedness revealed.

But bomber squadrons new visions see and drink fresh breath,
　　And penitence in failure (Our Lord's reprieve),
　　To fall there, patient in some foreign field.
Wised down, we locusts are Earth's grasshoppers again.

25 Return of the Magi

No epic suffices, not Homer's war and exploration,
    Not Vergil's empire, nor Dante's Church and state.
    For no one lifetime The Man's truth may create.
He came but once; no one world holds His incarnation.

    A man's part, evolution's mystery,
No lifetime plays, till he sees history as a whole.
Through Dark Wood was Dante's diary of the single soul,
    Perfected from violence, fraud and treachery.

Poet, connect! Shards draft no statement. No inspiration
    Sans hope affirms the firmaments await
    In star sweep. Presents presage past futures. So we
Magi, returning nowhere home, take home our role.

26 Marching to World Wars Memorial

(for Brigadier Claude Nicolson CB, 1898–1943)

'Say No to National Service,' the people says, who must
    Be right: now trust the peoples. The world's in pain.
    Come, Lingua Franca, mobilise amain
Ere sunset on English our Parliament, the world to trust.

    One world, one peoples, one Parliament – the core
Of faith: democracy but in one world may reign.
World's fiat of survival wasted turn round to gain.
    To martyrs' Civitas Dei restore

The acid test of death: accepted, their gold star dust.
    For naught but the Raising shall martyrdom sustain.
    Not fighting – you lose the right to fight! – costs more
Than losing the fight. So fight to lose and rise again!

27 Easter Island (*for Thor Heyerdahl*)

Case study for Gaia: Rapa Nui. Rats ate the palm seed
    From slash-and-burn. Slave traders brought disease.
    Their rafts had brought in rats with food seed for peace,
For slavers with human wickedness on them as rats to feed.

    Thor stone fields as wasted (volcanic with nutriment)
And Moai saw fallen (not dragged, they walked but sometimes
      fell).
Parent shows child why live, ancestors how – and tell
    On ahus standing where waters flow from vent.

Where Thor saw wars, relief from exhaustion was their need.
    Take hope for granted; let science man's living ease
    (Not with bare reason – with study applied well blent):
Earth's Easter Faith is care for the other: without, It's hell!

28 Not Paco

That boy I didn't know – bit of a lump – at tea,
    Who may be 12, plump, unattractive, I knew
    Needed to engage. . . He kissed me! What to do?
A stranger! 'Your name?' 'Don't know?' 'Then be for me maybe

    A Paco?' 'Why Spanish? More Greek-Italian.' 'So?'
'Who would I like to be?' The others leaving saw,
This was getting silly. I said, 'We must talk more,
    If ever we meet again. Now I must go.'

'I know,' said he, 'we shall . . .' (And so did I.) '. . . So we
    Must then do better.' 'How then know you?'
    'Not Paco. Best, know yourself. You're me!' 'No!' 'No . . ?'
'If still we cannot communicate,' I asked, 'What for?'

29 Hoopoe's Confession (*OW 23rd April 1973*)

Dear Wormwood, Felicitations on demotion, at expense
   Of Screwtape. You expect me: you are more absurd
   Than I am. I hurt myself – but spread His Word,
In hoping others may escape you. No defence –

   Not even consolation: I know It true!
A life of privilege to die for – and did not so;
A small poetic gift to hide behind, so as not to grow . . .
   Now all that's left me is a laugh at you.

Love's joy you never knew, nor yet the Vision Immense
   I had to betray, of beauty, art, Greek bird
   On Orchard lawn – and all spread out in dew
Of gratitude . . . And where that takes me, not yours to know.

30 Coplas por la Muerte de su Padre

(*in memory of GCW & Jorge Manrique*)

Shadows of kings and poets, Father, parade still through
   Your Hall, where tales fair of Empire I have heard.
   For some were slaves to valour and the Word,
Till history and language to their meanings left no clue.

   Respect for truth mines archaeology;
For lost ideas in shards their instinct recomposes,
While angry crowds fling ordure on our graveyard roses.
   Best rule, benevolent aristocracy:

Act worse, though, greed of the great they see than they could do,
   Knowing privilege abused worth scarce a turd.
   The scheme of least temptation, democracy –
Till Justice bids us resurrect the God of Moses.

To be a Pilgrim (*two douzets for TSE in admiration*)

31

No epic suffices, not Homer's war and exploration,
  Not Vergil's empire, not Dante's church and state.
  For no one lifetime the Man's truth may create:
He came but once; no one world grows His Incarnation.

  A man's a part of all that he may see,
All that of him. Not till history he sees as whole –
So may he not in one lifetime define his role –
  Shall he solve evolution's mystery.

Where he cannot be, ideas eternal for inspiration
  He navigates by, signosts of pilgrim's wait,
  Through Dark Wood (violence, fraud and treachery,
As backdrop). Dante's is journey of a single soul.

31 A

By language if obsessed, by imago not, il miglior fabbro
  Can be but obstacle to all but fame:
  Where worship impedes thought, what's in Its Name?
Through cultures, evolution is basso continuo . . .

  Ideas (words, music) as chemicals in blood
Build up each life Its personal identity.
Some, good or bad, do, some don't (not the Man, not you, not me)
  Degrade through successions, eras. We pray the good

With cultivation passed, while raised we onward go,
  As talisman bearing for ever unique the Same
  Man's icon – as members of the Body should,
In what we leave and take for perpetuity.

32 Hell (*for Dante Alighieri 1300 AD*)

How comfy! Lion, leopard, wolf – all in decline
    In Dark Wood (though not, man's greed and sins!) amid
    Iron donkeys, rigs and platforms . . . What am I bid
For weekend flight, gite, pool, coral prawns, blues, gold sunshine?

    Will Paradiso Terrestre for my Love do?
In back streets, drugs; asp under . . ? – scorpion! – . . . that stone:
She sees what I will not. She calls, calls; I postpone
    Postpone. And flux denied is vice: 'For you,

Long search – for Uebermensch . . .' Let instinct him define,
    Not Nature, that knows not how with Justice rid
    His beasts in man, and limits how construe
Which tempered mind as one with God and sins atone.

33 Purgatory (*for Brale Markovic 16vi*)

So hurry, scurry – before the Storm, folks' wandering
    And robot heaven: end time, best goals to score.
    Pose not for scenic history, castles, war –
Democracy's and NHS' ruins welcoming,

    Spent icons . . . Think what nimble apostles wear:
Their daily scrip, ring, diary, some coins and Testament?
What 'Nations' Unity', save Rome's blind fasces? They went,
    Sea swallows as neutrinos, too light to scare.

Across the universes, peace in one Raising:
    One Rule, work art for need and ask no more.
    Buffets but boosters: Justice in the air!
No bonds of empire – so time for the Lord's experiment.

34 Paradise (*for Papa 19vi*)

In quiet misery Pa sold the Hals: what good
    Love on our wall or Christ on Tree to kill?
    Then Norrington! The hall upon the hill
He had me see, to share grief selling. That's all he could.

    For Paradise is memory; so where
We were, we are – if once to truth we train the mind.
Once there inside, Pa nothing said, cruel to be kind?
    Or company mine, some Presence to help him bear?

Till sudden too he fell, great tree in Blackdown Wood,
    By Shipton's Stone. White Witch, bless too my will
    Space infinite to fill in heady air!
God everywhere: if here I could not, in heaven how find?

35 Divide and Rule

Its Power, the Kingdom, within you – a two-way street
    Across the earthquake chasm, none knows how spanned,
    Or what's the toll: your crossings need be planned;
Before we teleport, both sides in silence greet,

    Break codes and shadow box; as behind the screen,
Each t'other's puppet in spiritual exercise –
As athletes train for rising to the great surprise
    Of driving onward from where we have ever been.

All peoples need them: we have faith Olympiads will repeat,
    To purpose diverse events from every land –
    Work's festival of art and dance . . . The scene,
The duty cosmic, *but* unique seen through my eyes.

36 Duddings (for Papa's 108th)

(whose photo portrait 'Thinking of Finland' lives on the Duddings oak chair by Grampy's grandfather clock, next the Orchard Wyndham staircase hall gong)

Still memoirs save in deepest music I dare distrust,
    For images snatched, cropped tufts along the way.
    So Topsy would not trot from home away:
Home chatter inconsequential collects no dust . . .

    When Granny read me his Kipling, he through his door
Pretended not to listen, until – with wayward skill
Their Christopher thumped out the Grieg, and jealous will,
    To interrupt. Then Grampy's quiet awe

Gonged us to lunch. (He later gave me Arrau's; so I must
    Their Duddings scene remember.) For through play
    Truth speaks – as penguin chick's known call for more
Learns through It ocean flying. And Grampy calls me still.

37 Ealing Studios RIP

The terror is Terra Incognita! Fear not the door
    That slams behind man's follies, but leaves no peace.
    Duties come fresh with every moment and never cease.
Proud science predicts but past the event that instinct's before.

    The Raising's no holiday nor Holy Day.
Cheap, chick: man's Man His egg contains not; Sophia, respond!
This world laid waste, whole universes links life's bond.
    So mad my muddle, I'd never the Pilgrim's Way

Trudge on regardless, sans Faith's reluctant wit. The more
   St Simian's my nursery, I better ease
   My grief in bitter humour the next Last Day.
You, naughty child, are summoned by the Man beyond!

38 Poor Tom

I choose my friends like trees, because they're there till I
   Or *they* die. Oh, they have their secret nights
   As cats, mycelia though rooted in shrewd fights
And loves (beyond our ken, confabulations) – but sigh

   In winds, toss horse heads in my company.
Just so Tom was and is, in talk and memory,
Stern arguments and music: for friends are we,
   So indissoluble eternity.

Remember: universes in One Mercy fly,
   Though all as individual freedom flights:
   Where you or I happen in binary
On undiscovered thoughts, there I with you shall be.

For Tom

   Travel friend – Bayern, Rus, Corfu, Crete
   And in music and law so discrete:
      Since we were happy boys,
      We have shared griefs and joys –
   The foretaste of where next we meet.

39 Terra Cotta Robots

Death love in memories; in life love memory's wait!
    Qin-Mao-Xi broods terra cotta armies. We
    Instinct inconsequential follow, sans panoply
Or Fuehrer, huge duties in little kindnesses debate.

    Self worship total anchorite, their Fate.
Sealed workers deny for millennia grave robbers their story: the
      Whole
Is theirs, the God-Emperors'. AI plays safe each role
    (Wargames players, harems, acrobats, puppet state) –

While washing up we eternal travel contemplate.
    Dead robots, working ring-fenced their economy,
    Souls silly but democratic abominate.
Now lifeless their armies and godless – sans God's or a soul.

40 The Magic Flute (*for Picol @CWH 30vi24*)

('Der Vogelfanger bin ich, ja!')

Come read my lips from wind to pipe, the magic flute!
    Defining good in action is intimidation
    For oldies – nightmare confronting as poor relation,
To speak His Name – lest shame cut off Faith's tongue at root.

    For old age, no birds caged save ancient memory.
Be Word made flesh, kindness Itself: how dared I say,
My duty, as viaticum along my way,
    To live my library, so human be –

Were that not mandatory breath, as down Its chute
    This world falls flat, to hail His next Creation:
    So – useful, this martyr to absurdity!
Call second childhood for afterlife the Teacher's play.

41 Orchard Waters

House spring, monks' carp stew to Bridge-on-Willie, my last stand:
    New arboretum, a moment's permanence.
    The busy river contains the resonance
Of myriad voices, that goldcrest and dipper echo, from land

    To sea, in memory's single conversation –
Creation's icon to Saxon, Norman, Sir William
And back . . . The Avenue felled I hardly walk now, and ham,
    As loving Lear, their usurped conversation.

I have heard It all, and shall again, to understand
    In anamnesis wonder's step to sense,
    And Faith's to humility in shame – elation,
I am particle inalienably of His I AM!

42 Election Dreams

I'll die now (with ancient families decimated by World War)
    In Labour Raj (pro-Gaza, agin 'bedgate',
    MPs for themselves out as voters, the voters hate –
And boats of climate refugees along the shore.)

    Vote 'Change!' Change nothing but bury fear . . .
Folks' wandering in Planet wasted is necessity,
From fascist statism and Covid borrowings not free,
    We know, unless from earthy greed we tear

Ourselves in tears by Faith away to cosmic law . . .
    In train now to Pa, not Orchard, for him I wait,
    Rose give him, catch Grampy's cork popped: a tear
Each smiles, 'Plant roses in Raising – and build on memory'!

43 Parliament International On Air

Democracy is incremental: from Mother of Parliaments,
    To senate regional of countries, for Gaia
    Then up and over to all folks beyond and PIA.
Ambitious rulers require the People's common sense

    Well represented: assemblies petrify,
As state and leagues (trade, markets, NATO, UN) . . . Our planet,
Were worlds one Culture, would fail if needs outran it!
    Resource has survival none, save with oneness comply.

All law we know of universes is one, immense
    And pointilliste – and one in instinct's fire.
    So build and vote one Plan together, all – or die:
One Plan, with one consenting electorate to man It!

44 Postscript

Choose well your Fear: the rights of man Its management.
    Assume your Resurrection: then what's now?
    Love's Nature is one: God's would be won – but how?
Know then as now: live here, as trial to there were meant.

    As here sans love all's failure as death: there's fate.
My Fear of abandon: beginning of His wisdom. Dark Wood
In retrospect was trees: each led not to next. Life blood
    Is waters: greed's dread of motion must stagnate.

Fear life that's not then is betrayal: death's whole is soul's content.
    Know God there: here love's willingness allow.
    That could live even in a godless state:
Just Fear's not of being here a failure – for there of just not
    being good.

45 From Heraclitus to Plato (*for Lucy*)

(ΑΝΩ ΚΑΙ ΚΑΤΩ 'ΟΔΟΣ - ΑΡΧΗ ΑΝΥΠΟΘΕΤΟΣ)

Come build your twin-isms from the bottom up; from dirt
   To bully to the vulgar compromise:
   Vox populi, vox dei, your human eyes!
Both communist and fascist, from their need and hurt,

   Come build: all but you choosing is the same.
Conceal yourself like caddis, octopus or snail,
Your within growing as universal as ocean whale.
   Take all, love all: It is the sacred game.

Vote as you will or shout: you can but bet your shirt.
   If wise and kind, from shapeless clay you rise,
   Self-made from instinct, your unsuspected Name –
Way up, way down, each yourself sure, though both shall fail.

In the Olive Garden

(*cosmic resurrection for Humphrey, Adriana and Elle*)

   Eternal prayer of City, bird and tree;
   Dawn in an olive garden kneeling,
   Dawn nestling in that hoopoe's crest:
   Dawn overlooks the City and forgets . . .

   Old men – and olives too – are history,
   Do not communicate, their fruiting
   More subtle. Unknown, unknowing tests
   The hoopoe – chooses her proper tree and nests.

'The Road is in You', defines your common cosmic end –
    Each particle One Body's evolution.
    Each death scrapes off a skin of your pollution.
Already is outgrown, Homunculus, this Earth's waste to defend.

    But one by one again, again, your pilgrim course
Together, till body and mind, in royal free Assumption
Fused, overcome your adolescent despond's presumption
    Of final failure from every mean folly, war and loss!

No peace sans justice; no rest on death. So tasks impend –
    Tough love: rough work is your healing absolution!
    God's gravity raise to good your last resumption:
One Will perfects to stasis His Coriolis Force!

    Humanist chimneys
    Refute evolution: no
    Wake at friends' raising?

47 No Justice

No justice to find in underworlds, where He foresees
    Sans mercy the evil His men choose. I fear
    No hell I am not created to forestall; revere
No Lord, hold dear no heaven, where Earth is His disease:

    In bogeys and bullies, humbug and horrors, no shame –
So no redemption . . . Yet glories and mysteries and beauties,
      the fun
Of truth in things, oh and think the type of billions in the sun!
    On each writ small, the Rule but frees one Name,

At birth given googolplex from singularity's
    Deep freeze on pain of loving repentance, so dear
    It cost God life, in loss to win His Game.
No death's escape, but challenge thrown down again begun!

        Justice eternal:
    Let's not from contempt of hell
      Despair of heaven!

Love You I could not more than You gave me to love
    Myself, nor more conceive, dear Whipping Boy . . .
    Thence rules define; that asymptote employ –
Just so, know how I'd be, Lord, on Your Hand Your glove:

    Just so there feeling conscience' absurdity!
I, every I, must rise so high as You, to stoop so low –
Your peregrine for Ganymede, we all? Just so,
    To make me low, as You make You next me?

I kindness dwindle, with Gaia's resources, to prove
    Here evolution's limits and pilgrim fruits enjoy.
    How measure such eternal purgatory –
Live how many lives, Your joy of loving at last to show?

William Wyndham, Transfiguration,
Orchard Wyndham 2024